BLACK+DECKER

The Complete Guide to
TREEHOUSES

Updated 2nd Edition

Design & Build Your Kids a Treehouse

COOL
SPRINGS
PRESS

First published in 2012 by Cool Springs Press, an imprint of The Quarto Group, 100 Cummings Center, Suite 265-D, Beverly, MA 01915, USA. T (978) 282-9590 F (978) 283-2742 QuartoKnows.com

20

ISBN 978-1-58923-661-5

Library of Congress Cataloging-in-Publication Data on file

President/CEO: Ken Fund
Group Publisher: Bryan Trandem

Home Improvement Group

Associate Publisher: Mark Johanson
Managing Editor: Tracy Stanley
Developmental Editor: Jordan Wiklund

Creative Director: Michele Lanci
Art Direction/Design: Brad Springer, James Kegley, Kim Winscher, Brenda Canales

Staff

Lead Photographer: Corean Komarec
Set Builder: James Parmeter
Production Managers: Laura Hokkanen, Linda Lund

Author: Philip Schmidt
Page Layout Artist: Danielle Smith
Technical Editor: Eric Smith
Shop Help: Charles Boldt

Printed in China

Contents

The Complete Guide
to Treehouses

Contents (Cont.)

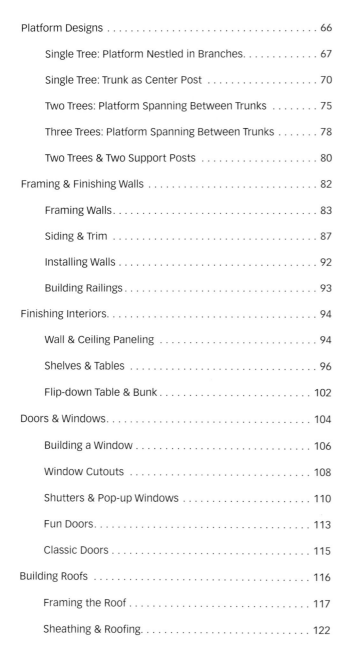

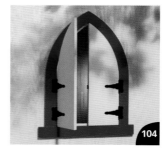

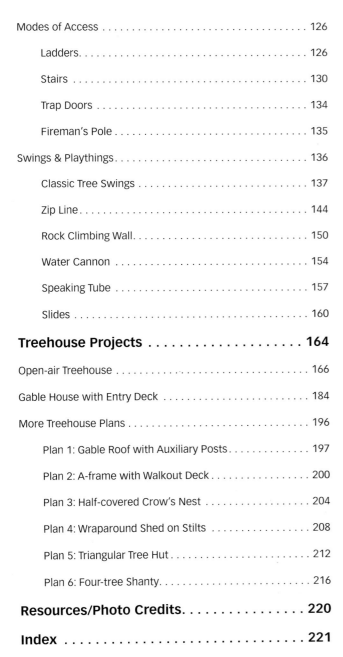

Introduction

A treehouse may be the truest example of "living" space. For kids, it's a room that never has to be cleaned, a place for muddy shoes and bug jars and adventures real and imagined; a house that you can paint whenever and however you want, without gaining approval. For adults, it's a room that never has to be cleaned, a place for muddy shoes and…well, you get the idea. But best of all a treehouse is up in a tree. And that's just cool.

If you're fortunate enough to have a yard with at least one sizable tree on it, you've probably entertained the idea of building a treehouse (after all, you are human, which makes you roughly 96 percent chimp). So what's stopping you? Let's see…you're not a carpenter, your design skills are largely or totally untested, and you don't know the first thing about building a house, let alone one that hovers 10 feet above the ground. No big deal—you can do this.

The first step is to learn a little bit about trees and decide whether you have a suitable host. And don't worry if your yard isn't blessed with the perfect specimen; there are plenty of options for the arboreally challenged. Next comes a basic lesson in treehouse design (if you can tell the difference between a 2 × 4 and a lag screw, you'll do just fine). Here you'll also learn the important relationship between the tree and the house design and why the living wood determines the best plan for the lumber.

The foundation of any treehouse is the platform. That's what's anchored to the tree and therefore requires the most specialized techniques and considerations. But once the platform is in place, a treehouse goes up pretty much like any outdoor building, such as a shed or a doghouse for an Irish Wolfhound. Yet treehouses aren't just tree-borne outbuildings; many of them are more like out-there buildings, with funky angles, fun accessories, and all manner of custom details that sprout from the builder's imagination or, more accurately, from their inner child. Zip line, anyone?

Whatever you can dream up, this book will help you build it. You'll be talked and walked through each part of the process so that all that's left is adding your own design ideas and inspiration from others (kids in particular). Most treehouse builders find that creating a house is as much fun as playing in one. If this holds true for you, we'll probably see you back here again when it's time to put on an addition or to break bark on your second home.

Lofty Ideas

Just as no two trees are exactly alike, no two treehouses are precisely the same in every detail. In fact, you'll find as much if not more variety among houses in trees as you'll find among the trees themselves. This diversity of design has a lot to do with diversity of builders. Treehouses tend to inspire our innate creativity and grant us license to have fun in a way that terrestrial houses and garages don't. On the following few pages you'll find a stunning portfolio that is a testament to the diversity and creativity that surround the treehouse. From bright and whimsical to subdued and relaxed, you'll find a wealth of themes, motifs, styles, and ideas that will inform and inspire you in your treehouse pursuit.

The bigger the tree the more options you'll have for designing and attaching a treehouse. Here, a colorful lookout tower with a ramp and climbing net piggybacks onto one side of a mature oak tree.

Vibrant colors and fun shapes add whimsy and playfulness to this treehouse, which also features a unique limb penetration through a sidewall.

Treehouses and spaceships often share some design features, contributing to the out-of-this-world appeal of a fort in the trees. Despite appearances, the structure beneath this treehouse is a shed, not an outhouse. (But if it were an outhouse, note that the builder sited it, appropriately, beneath the treehouse, not above it.)

A secret garden in the trees will delight and charm anyone, providing fertile ground for storybook dreams.

Rustic appeal is created by using logs and limbs instead of lumber to build your treehouse. Be aware, though, that some municipalities may not allow this practice.

Build your own door to capture precisely the feeling you want your treehouse to put forth. (Besides, a treehouse is no place for fancy manufactured millwork you buy from the design store.)

A treehouse can become part of a tree. By following the flow of the tree limbs as you design and build, you may find that the tree steers you in intriguing directions.

Keeping it simple is a solid approach to treehouse design. A plain treehouse is a blank slate for the imagination.

Four seasons of fun can be enjoyed in your treehouse, as long as your coats and mittens are up to the task.

Extra support from a set of posts can let you install a relatively large treehouse in a relatively small tree.

A pair of trees roughly the same size provide solid support for a treehouse that's nestled between them.

Common house styles can be adapted to your treehouse design with pleasing effect, as with the chalet-inspired treehouse seen here.

"House" can mean many things in a tree. A roof may be a canopy of branches and a wall could be bright boards and string. Do check with your local building department before following your fancy too far, however. The rope railings seen here would be red-flagged by a lot of inspectors.

A climbing net and a sturdy platform in a sprawling tree spell big fun for one lucky family.

A treehouse is a fortress of fun even with siding from bark slabs and a tar paper roof. In fact, these simple materials have a beauty all their own that many designers find appealing.

With a platform in place, a tree structure is ready for use. You may wish to add walls and a roof as you go to spread out the work and allow you to adapt to actual needs and preferences as your kids grow.

A treehouse has an inside, too, and like the exterior it can be as simple or as complex as you choose. The photos on this page depict a treehouse that's definitely on the more finished side, with sleeping bunks, hardwood flooring, and even electricity.

An elevated house in the trees with an independent post support system has the appeal of a tree-built treehouse but without many of the structural limitations.

What better place for a dreamy deck than outside the front door of your treehouse?

Shingle siding and a compact Cape Cod design lend the flavor of old Nantucket to this treehouse (even though it happens to be located in Saint Paul, Minnesota).

An enclosed staircase inside the adjoining fort provides sheltered access to the gangway and the lookout perch.

If all the world's indeed a stage, this tree-based theater/playhouse fits right in (and what a perfect venue for the Neighborhood Kid Players production).

A well-designed, well-built treehouse can completely change your outlook on growing up.

Measure the circumference of potential host trees for your treehouse to determine if the tree is big enough for the job. To support a treehouse, a single tree should be at least 5 ft. in circumference.

Treehouse Basics

The design process for treehouses is often a bit more freewheeling than it may be for terrestrial structures. In fact, the traditional way to design a treehouse (and a technique still used frequently today) is basically to climb up into a tree with boards and fasteners and start to build, making it up as you go along. One of the great attributes of treehouses is that there are very few rules. But the rules that do exist are important ones. And even experienced treehouse builders spend time up-front learning the rules, assessing the needs of the treehouse occupants and performing one of the most critical design tasks: choosing the best tree.

In this chapter:

- Choosing a Tree
- Planning & Design
- Treehouse Safety

Family D-I-Y ▶

If you're building a treehouse for kids to use or share with the adults, include them in the design process. Many a parent has gone to great lengths to surprise kids with a fancy treehouse that ultimately doesn't get used. It's like gifting a young child with an exquisite toy only to find that their favorite part is the ribbon on the box.

Not only will kids get more pleasure from a house they help to create, but by finding practical solutions to bring their creative ideas to life, they also will learn the essence of architecture. Who knows, you might have another Frank Lloyd Wright on your hands, or better yet for treehouses, another Christopher Wren.

Encourage creativity by soliciting ideas from all of your family members and try to work the ideas into the final plan.

Choosing a Tree

Daydreaming aside, finding your host tree is the first real step in the treehouse process. This is because the tree will have the most say in the final design of the treehouse. More ambitious treehouse plans require healthier trees. In the end, if your host tree isn't up to the task, you'll have to consider a smaller treehouse or figure in some posts for structural support.

Lots of treehouses are hosted by multiple trees. This is usually a good idea from a strength standpoint. However, designing the house can be a lot like working by committee, since trees, like people, tend to act independently when the going gets tough.

For most treehouse builders, the selection process isn't a question of which tree to use but rather, "Will old Barkey in our backyard support a treehouse?" For them, the health test is crucial. You don't want to kill your one, beloved tree by burdening it with a temporary structure.

This chapter provides some general tips and rules to help you find a suitable host for your dream house. But before you start, there's this advice (it won't be the last time you hear it): When in doubt, ask an arborist. They're in the phone book, they're not expensive, and they can advise you on everything from tree diagnosis to healthy pruning to long-term maintenance.

General Tree Health

A tree doesn't have to be in the absolute prime of its life to be a suitable host, but it must be healthy. Asking a tree how it's been feeling lately probably won't teach you much, so you have to take a holistic approach by piecing together some standard clues. Other factors, such as location, can rule out a candidate more decisively.

AGE

Mature trees are best. They're bigger, stronger, and move less in the wind than young ones. They also have more heartwood (the hard, inner core of dead wood). When you drive a lag screw into a tree, it's the heartwood that really offers gripping power.

ROOTS

For some reason people don't like the sight of exposed roots at the base of a tree. So they cover them with dirt and flower beds. This is like burying someone at the beach and forgetting to stop at their neck. It suffocates the tree roots and can affect the health of the whole tree. If your tree's root flares are buried from re-grading or gardening, take it as a warning sign that there might be problems below.

Another thing to check for is girdling, where newer roots—often from nearby plants—have grown around the tree's primary anchoring roots, cutting off their life supply. Trees next to unpaved driveways or heavily trodden paths may have suffered damage from all the traffic; another warning sign.

To make sure your tree's foundation stays healthy, don't grow grass or add soil over the root flares. Keep shrubs and other competing plants outside of the ground area defined by the reach of the branches. And by all means, keep cars and crowds off the base roots, especially on trees with shallow root systems (see Choosing a Tree Species, on page 27).

TRUNK, BRANCHES & LEAVES (OR NEEDLES)

Inspect the largest members of the tree—the trunk and main branches. Look for large holes and hollow spots, rot on the bark or exposed areas, and signs of bug infestation. Check old wounds and damaged areas to see how the tree is healing. Avoid trees with a significant lean, as they are more likely to topple in a storm.

Trees with multiple trunks often are fine for building in; however, the trunk junction is vulnerable to being pulled apart, especially under the added stress of a treehouse. The recommended remedy for this is to bind the tree up above with cables to prevent the trunks from spreading. This is a job for an arborist.

When it comes to branches, look for stout limbs that meet the trunk at a near-perpendicular angle. Typically, the more acute the angle, the weaker the connection, although several suitable tree species naturally have branches set at 45°. Dead branches here and there typically aren't a problem. These can, and should, be cut off before you start building.

Finally, look at the canopy. In spring and summer the leaves should be green and full with no significant bare spots. Needles on evergreen trees should look normal and healthy.

Watch Your Waste Wood ▶

When you're building the treehouse and drilling holes for anchor screws, pay attention to the wood chips pulled out by the bit: granulated, dusty material indicates rot inside the tree and should be investigated further. Look for clean spirals and tough flakes or chips.

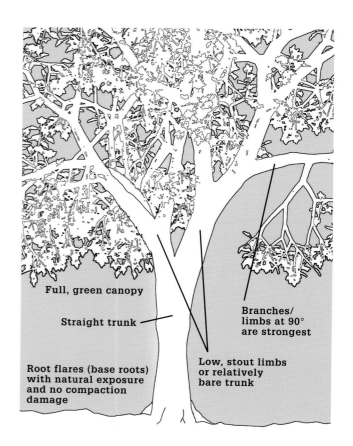

Full, green canopy

Straight trunk

Branches/ limbs at 90° are strongest

Root flares (base roots) with natural exposure and no compaction damage

Low, stout limbs or relatively bare trunk

Is It Big Enough?

Well, that depends on how big a house you want. The truth is, in the end, you'll have to be the judge of what your tree can safely support. Here are some general guidelines for assessing tree size, assuming the tree is mature and healthy and the treehouse is a moderately sized (100 square feet or so), one-story affair:

- A single tree that will be the sole support for the house should measure at least five feet in circumference at its base.

- Main supporting limbs (where each limb supports one corner of the house's platform) should be at least 6" in diameter (19" circumference).
- The bigger the tree, the less it will move in the wind, making it a more stable support for a treehouse.
- Different types and shapes of trees have different strength characteristics—a professional's assessment of your tree can help you plan accordingly.

Building in a group of trees is a good way to provide adequate support for a treehouse, but it comes with the added challenge of dealing with multiple forces and directional movement.

Location

Other important considerations for siting your treehouse are where the tree sits on your property and what sits around the tree. The wrong location can immediately rule out a tree as a good host.

Let's start with the neighbors. If the tree is too close to your neighbor's property line, thus making your treehouse all too visible, they might complain to the authorities. Soon there's a guy on your doorstep with one of those official-looking metal clipboard boxes full of citation papers and other things you hate to see your name on. Of course, your neighbors might not care what you do, but it's best to talk with them now rather than later. Also, building too close to your property line may involve the authorities simply because you're breaking setback laws of the local zoning code (see page 29).

Trees located on a steep hillside may be too stressed already to handle the added weight and wind resistance of a treehouse. Likewise, trees at water's edge are likely to be unstable and may be fighting a constant battle with erosion.

Treehouses in plain view of roads, paths, or other public byways are begging for trouble because people are fascinated by treehouses. Motorists driving by might be distracted, and kids and teenagers walking by may be tempted to explore (or trash) the house.

Other hazards to look for: nearby power lines or utility poles, roofs or chimneys that come close to the treehouse site, and fences and other potentially dangerous obstacles in the "fall line" underneath the treehouse. Any parent knows how creatively kids court danger. Try not to make it too easy for them.

What to Look For

Avoid trees near roads and busy pathways. Cars, kids, and pets don't always mix well.

Trees tend to grow. Take into consideration the proximity of utility lines.

Trees close to water are vulnerable to erosion and will require constant adult supervision. Consider trees that have a fence between children and water.

Behavior

How your tree acts when the wind blows will become a critical factor in many of your design decisions. That's why, at this selection stage, it's wise to rule out any tree that moves too much. You should never try to weather a storm from inside a treehouse. However, the house itself has no choice but to stay put.

Get to know the tree. If there's a wild branch that likes to swing like a scythe in the wind, you'll have to plan around it, restrain it in a healthy manner, or (if necessary) chop it off. The problem of high winds is only compounded when you build in multiple trees where independent movement of individual trees can exert some nasty opposing forces on your little dream house. Tree movement is a basic reality of treehouse construction, and there are effective methods for dealing with it. The more you know about the tree, the better you can design your house to get along with its host in all conditions.

Treeschool ▸

As a treehouse builder, it's important to understand the inner workings of your benevolent host. This not only builds respect for some of nature's oldest living things, it will also help you decide the best and healthiest ways to build in the tree—where to place screws, support cables, posts, etc. And yes, there may be a quiz.

TREE ANATOMY

All eyes to the illustration at right. Now then, a tree trunk and branches have four main layers. The innermost layer is the heartwood, made of dead cells that form a hard, strong core that helps support the tree. Next, the sapwood is living fibrous tissue that carries sap (water and nutrients) from the roots to the leaves. Surrounding the sapwood is a thin layer of growing tissue called the cambium. It helps develop new wood and the inner bark layer. Finally, the bark is the outer layer of dead cells that protects the inner layers. Underneath the familiar rough layer of bark (called cork) is a soft inner bark—the phloem— which carries food from the leaves to the rest of the tree.

As you can see, the tree's main food supply channels lie close to the surface. That's why you must minimize any damage to the outer layers. Removing the bark exposes the tree to infection, while cutting into the phloem layer stops the vertical flow of food. One of the worst things you can do to a tree is to cut a ring around the trunk or a branch, or even bind it tightly with rope or cable. This stops all circulation to the rest of the tree.

HOW A TREE GROWS

A tree grows taller through the ends of the trunk and branches. That means that big lower limbs—the kind that are good supports for houses—stay at the same elevation. Trunks and branches also grow in diameter, thanks to the cambium. How much growth depends on the tree, but as a general rule, always leave a 1 to 2" gap around tree parts when encircling them with framing and decking.

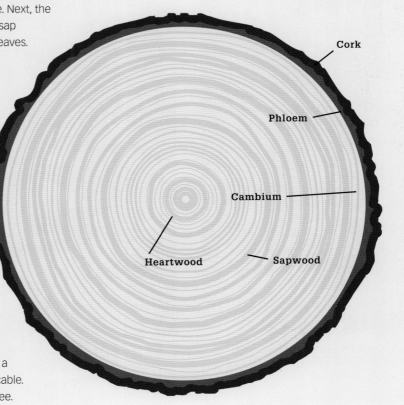

Cork

Phloem

Cambium

Heartwood

Sapwood

Grooming the Winner

Once you've selected the best candidate, it's time to get it prettied up for the big event. A routine pruning is a good idea, but don't start hacking off healthy limbs to make room for a backyard McMansion (see Proper Pruning, below). Get rid of dead branches in the tree and clear the ground underneath. If you'd like a soft ground cover beneath (a recommended kid-safety measure), cover the area with several inches of wood chips, preferably from the same species of tree. Don't cover the area with soil.

Later, when you have a better idea of the size of your treehouse, make sure the structure won't be blocking the roots' source of rainwater. If it will, find out how much and how often you'll need to water the tree to compensate.

Proper Pruning ▸

The best tool for pruning is a telephone. Use it to call an arborist and have them assess the tree and make the appropriate cuts. If you do decide to go it alone, be careful, and follow these basic rules:

1.   Never cut away more than ⅓ of the tree's branches.
2.   Start with a shallow undercut several inches away from the branch bark collar—the bulge where the branch meets the trunk. The undercut ensures the bark doesn't peel off as the branch drops.
3.   Complete the cut from the top to remove the bulk of the branch.
4.   Make a final cut flush with the outside of the branch bark collar. Do not cut into the collar.
5.   Leave the wound to heal itself. Don't paint it or add any kind of sealant or preservative.

Start by undercutting from beneath the limb with your bow saw or chain saw.

Finish the cut from above—this keeps the bark from tearing when the limb breaks loose.

Trim the stub from the limb so it's flush with the branch collar.

Choosing a Tree Species

GOOD TREES

DECIDUOUS (BROADLEAF) TREES

	Characteristics	Native Area	Average Height
Oak	Strong, durable, low branches	**Black Oak:** California, eastern US	30-80 ft.
		White Oak: eastern US	50-90 ft.
		Live Oak: California, Texas, southern US	40-50 ft.
		Northern Red: central and eastern US into Canada	60-80 ft.
Maple	**Sugar Maple** is preferred over **Red**, but both are good hosts	**Sugar Maple:** northeastern US, north into Canada	60-80 ft.
		Red Maple: eastern half of US, north into Canada	50-70 ft.
Beech	Smooth bark, horizontal branches	Eastern US, southeastern Canada	60-80 ft.
Apple	Low, stout branches	Most of US, southern Canada	20-30 ft.
Ash	Strong, straight trunk; should be checked for good health	Eastern half of US, southeastern Canada	60-80 ft.

EVERGREEN (NEEDLELEAF) TREES

	Characteristics	Native Area	Average Height
Douglas Fir	Long-living; large, mature trunks have few low branches	Pacific coast, US and Canadian Rocky Mountains	180-250 ft.
Pine	Fast-growing; branches often numerous but small and flexible	**Ponderosa Pine:** western half of US, British Columbia	100-180 ft.
		Eastern White Pine: northeastern, Great Lakes, and Appalachian regions of US	75-100 ft.
		Sugar Pine: California, Oregon, western Nevada	175-200 ft.
Spruce	Can be prone to infestation; shallow roots	**Black Spruce:** Alaska, Canada, northeastern US	30-40 ft.
		Engelmann Spruce: Pacific Northwest, Rocky Mountain states	100-120 ft.
Hemlock	Immature trees may have little trunk exposure	Great Lakes and Appalachian regions of US, southeastern Canada	60-75 ft.

NOT-SO-GOOD TREES

DECIDUOUS TREES	DRAWBACKS
Cottonwood	Soft, spongy wood
Birch	Short lifespan, weak branches
Poplar & Aspen	Shallow roots, short lifespan
Black Walnut	Branches are brittle and break easily

Planning & Design

If you built a treehouse as a kid you probably didn't spend a lot of time planning it beforehand. You had plenty of ideas and knew what you wanted—a trap door, a lookout post, a tire swing, and maybe a parachuting platform or helicopter pad—you just weren't exactly sure how everything would come together. In the end, you decided to figure it out along the way and got started.

Of course, some people might use the same approach today (good luck on the helicopter pad), but be advised that a little planning up front could save your project from disaster. Remember the guy with the metal clipboard from the city office? You don't want him showing up with a demolition order just as you're nailing up the last piece of trim.

This chapter will get you thinking about general design features, such as the size and style of the treehouse, where it will sit in the tree, and how you'll get from the ground to the front door—if you want a front door. In this section we cover the all-important construction details, like anchoring to the tree and building the platform, walls, and roof. Inevitably there's plenty of give-and-take between design dreams and structural necessity. But that's what makes treehouse building such a fun and satisfying challenge.

Note: Before refining your treehouse plans, see Treehouse Safety (page 50) for important safety-related design considerations.

Planning and designing a treehouse is a fun, instructive activity that everyone in the family can enjoy.

Building Codes & Zoning Laws

It's time to pinch your nose and swallow the medicine. The sooner you get it over with, the sooner you can go out and play. By checking into the building and zoning rules for your area you can avoid the mistake of spending time on elaborate plans only to run into a brick wall of bureaucracy.

When it comes to building codes and treehouses, the official word is that there is no official word. Many municipalities—the governing powers over building and zoning laws—consider treehouses to be "temporary" structures when they fit within certain size limits, typically about 100 to 120 square feet and not more than 10 to 12 feet tall. If you have concerns about the restrictiveness of the local laws, keeping your treehouse within their size limits for temporary structures is a good precaution to take.

It's often likely that city officials consider treehouses too minor to be concerned with them. On top of that, building codes for earth-bound buildings are based on measurable, predictable factors that engineers use to calculate things like strength requirements. Drafting a set of standards for structures built on living, moving, and infinitely variable foundations (trees) quickly becomes a cat-herding exercise for engineers. Thus, few codes exist that set construction standards for treehouses. This means more responsibility is placed on the builder.

When it comes to zoning laws, the city planning office is concerned less with a treehouse's construction and more with its impact on your property. They may state that you can't build anything within 3 feet or more of your property line (a setback restriction) or that you can't build a treehouse in your front yard (the Joneses might not be the treehouse type).

The bottom line is this: Your local planning office might require you to get a building permit and pass inspections for your treehouse, or they might not care what you do, provided you keep the building within specific parameters. It's up to you to learn the rules.

Some of the elements that may be regulated by your local building code and zoning laws include:

- Size restriction (square footage of floor plan).
- Height restriction (from the ground to the top of the treehouse).
- Setback (how closely you can build to the property line).
- Railing height and baluster spacing.

Although city laws are all over the place regarding treehouses, here are a few tips that might help you avoid trouble with your treehouse:

- Talk with your neighbors about your treehouse plans. A show of respect and diplomacy on your part is likely to prevent them from filing a complaint with the authorities. It also smooths the way for later when you have to borrow tools for the project.
- Be careful where you place windows (and decks) in your treehouse. Your neighbors might be a touch uncomfortable if you suddenly have a commanding view of their hot tub or a straight shot into their second-story windows.
- Electricity and, especially, plumbing services running to a treehouse tell the authorities that you plan to live there, which means your house crosses a big line from "temporary structure" to "residence" or "dwelling" and becomes subject to all the requirements of the standard building code.
- Don't build in a front-yard tree or any place that's easily viewed from a public road. The point is not to hide from the authorities, it's that conspicuous treehouses attract too much attention for the city's comfort, and the house might annoy your neighbors.
- In addition to keeping the size of your house in check, pay attention to any height restriction for backyard structures. Treehouses can easily exceed these, for obvious reasons, but nevertheless may be held to the same height limits as sheds and garages.
- Even if the local building laws don't cover treehouses, you can look to the regular building code for guidance. It outlines construction standards for things like railings, floor joist spans, and accommodations for local weather and geologic (earthquake) conditions. With appropriate adaptations for the treehouse environment, many of the standards established for ground-houses will work for your perched palace.

Elements of a Treehouse

Treehouses can range in style from miniature versions of traditional houses to funky masterpieces of original inspiration. Of course, your ideal treehouse might be nothing more than a lofty hammock slung above a pine deck. Personal taste is what it's all about. Here are some design options to get you thinking.

WALLS

Walls define the look and shape of a house and do more than any other element to create the feel of the interior space. A treehouse can have solid walls for privacy and a greater sense of enclosure, or it can open up to the elements and let the tree define its boundaries. If you'd like both options, consider an awning-style wall with a hinged top section that flips open.

Enclosed walls, either full height or stub walls like these, block or partially block views into the neighbors' yard and create a secret room for kids.

Open walls admit breezes and allow unobstructed views, plus they're easier and cheaper to build than enclosed walls. If you choose not to build walls, build safety railings instead.

Flip-up panels let you open up a section of the wall or roof for airflow when you don't need to batten down for shelter.

Round or curved walls blend naturally with the shape of a tree.

ROOFS

Treehouse roofs can take on almost any shape and often exhibit a combination of styles. Incorporating branches and trunks into the roof design makes for interesting, organic forms. A common approach to designing a roof is to start with a traditional style then improvise as needed to fit your house. Or, you might decide to skip the roof altogether, preferring the shelter of the tree's canopy rather than boards and shingles.

Shed roofs have an easy-to-build, flat shape, making them a good choice for all types of treehouses.

Gable roofs are considered the most classic roof style, with angled wall sections at either end.

A removable roof made from canvas or a plastic tarp may be all you need to shelter a tree fort or sun deck.

Hip roofs are sloped on all sides and are more difficult to frame than sheds and gables.

A conical roof is an impressive way to top a rounded wall. They're built with closely spaced rafters fanning out from the roof peak.

WINDOWS & DOORS

The best doors and windows to use on treehouses are either found or homemade. It's fun to design a wall or entryway around salvaged materials—maybe a reclaimed ship's porthole window or a creaky old cellar door. You could use new, factory-made units, but their large size and polished appearance don't fit most treehouses. Kids especially love playful designs, such as Dutch doors, with swinging top and bottom halves, or little peek-a-boo openings through which they can demand, "Who goes there?!"

Architectural salvage shops are full of interesting finds for windows and doors.

Simple homemade windows are easy to make with plastic glazing and scrap lumber.

Dutch doors offer a fun change of pace that kids (and adults) find charming.

A solid door with a padlock or bolt latch may be a good idea, if not necessary, for securing a remote treehouse.

ACCESS OPTIONS

Perhaps the best thing about a treehouse is all the cool stuff that you can't have in a real house, like trap doors and cargo nets and fireman's poles. And who needs a front door when you can exit SWAT-style down a climbing rope? Okay, not everyone is the right age for the ninja lifestyle. A sturdy ladder or even a staircase are also perfectly respectable modes for accessing a treehouse. But just to be safe you might want to include a secret escape hatch and zip line...in case of an alien air assault.

Ladders provide safe and easy access while maintaining a sense of remoteness.

Stairs are a good, practical option for multi-use and multi-user treehouses.

DECKS

One of the most popular treehouse designs includes a house covering about ½ to ⅔ of its supporting platform, leaving the rest open for a small deck or sitting porch. This is a nice way to provide both open and enclosed spaces for your lofty getaway. A small deck in front makes a good, safe landing for a staircase or access ladder, while a large deck can be the perfect spot for having a drink with friends at sunset.

Centering a small house on a platform makes an instant wraparound deck.

With the platform in place, it's easy to make room for a tree deck.

Stairs or a ladder require a top landing; adding a foot or two of space to the landing lets it double as a sitting area.

Design Considerations

Ask any treehouse nut about design and you're bound to be advised to let the tree lead the way. This means respecting the tree's natural strengths and weaknesses and not over-stressing it with an unsuitable or excessive house design. It also speaks to aesthetics. Much of a treehouse's appeal comes from its host, and the best house designs complement the tree's character or make use of special natural features. Designing within the branches, as it were, is also good treehouse philosophy and makes the planning and construction—not to mention the enjoyment—of your house as fun as it should be.

So, now that you've picked a tree and had a talk with the folks at the local planning office, it's time to give your house some shape; in your mind at least. As you mull over the height, size, and features of your new home, don't be afraid to make sketches of your ideas—despite what we've all been told, doodling during work is actually a good thing. This will also help with the final step of the design process—making scaled drawings.

PLATFORM HEIGHT

The first big decision to make is how high to set the treehouse. If it will be used by kids, keep the platform no more than six to eight feet above the ground. Any higher is dangerous, and kids will have just as much

fun at six feet as they would at 12 or 20 feet If your treehouse is designed mostly for adults, you can go higher, but before deciding ask yourself:

- Will you need easy access? If you're using the house as an office or studio, consider the difficulty of hauling up supplies (and lunch).
- Is construction feasible? Building a treehouse is generally the most potentially hazardous aspect of treehouse life. Also, construction could be slowed considerably by a very high platform.
- Will neighborhood kids be able to climb up into the house? If so, you could be courting trouble with a lofty placement.

Regardless of where you build, you must make sure the treehouse placement is good for the tree. Arborists recommend building below the tree's center of gravity. This is something you'll just have to get a feel for, based on the tree's size and behavior. One general guideline is to build in the lowest ⅓ of the tree's overall height. If you're lucky, your host tree will make it easy for you and have a perfect open cradle of stout limbs at just the right height. Alas, it's usually not that obvious.

Another consideration is pruning the tree to make room for your house. While thoughtful, therapeutic

It doesn't take much elevation for kids to get that lofty feeling in their own treehouse.

Don't use the familiar nailed-on steps for access. They can easily give way to the side or pull completely out of the tree while you're climbing.

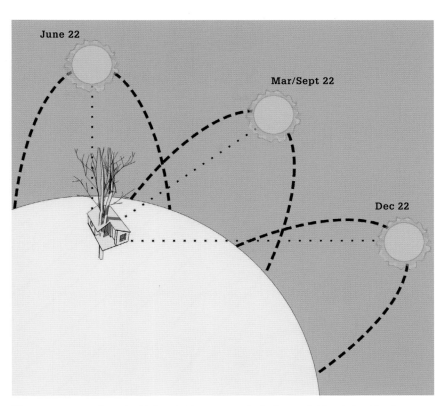

June 22

Mar/Sept 22

Dec 22

The sun moves from its high point in summer to its low point in winter. Shadows change accordingly. Try and keep the sun in mind as you plan.

pruning is good, and recommended by tree experts, removing large, healthy limbs to pave the way for easy construction is really straying from the point of building in a tree. If an obstructing limb becomes a deal-breaker for your house plans, consult an arborist to make sure that removing it won't harm the tree.

Finally, give yourself a good, old fashioned visual reference: Climb up in the tree (or onto a ladder) and stand at the proposed platform height. Check out the view and the headroom. Picture yourself lounging like there's no tomorrow. Happy? Good. Now you can decide how to get from the ground to your finished house.

ACCESS

To help determine the means of access, look again to the users of the treehouse. Older—that is, mature—people probably would prefer stairs or a comfortable ladder, while kids usually want a more challenging or fun route (just say no to mini-tramps and pole vaulting, however). Do you want a ladder or stairs that are easy to reach from your regular house? Or out of view from the house?

Make sure your planned means of access is viable for the chosen platform height. One mode of access to rule out: steps or rungs individually fastened along the tree trunk. Even when built properly—with threaded screws, not nails—these are fraught with safety problems and require an unnecessary amount of hardware placed into the tree.

SUN & SEASONS

As with a regular house, sunlight and weather are important design considerations. Perhaps you've dreamed of waking up with the summer sunrise or climbing into your perch to catch the sunset after a long day at the office. Position your house carefully to make the most of your favorite outdoor hours. For kids, some full shade is a must to avoid prolonged sun exposure.

With deciduous trees, the changing seasons come with a potential shocker. When fall hits and your host tree is suddenly a bare skeleton, your treehouse might stick out like an embarrassing tattoo. Just something to keep in mind if you're building when the tree's canopy is full.

Two walls or railings and two tape measures make it easy to visualize floor space you'll need in your new treehouse.

SIZE, SHAPE & PROPORTIONS

Think small. Or at least start by thinking small. Here's why: Weight is an important factor for any treehouse. The larger the house, the greater the weight burden on the tree. A big house will also catch more wind, stressing the branches more than they're used to and generally making it harder for the tree to stay upright. It's not unheard of to have a disproportionately large treehouse create such a windsail that the entire tree blows over. If you feel the need to go big, find a big tree or build in a group of very stable trees.

In treehouses, wall heights don't need to be the standard 8 feet that they are in regular houses. For adults, 6½ feet is a better place to start. This makes the house cozier and more nest-like. The necessary headroom for a kids' treehouse depends on their ages and how long they're likely to use the house. Generally, 6 feet of headroom should give them plenty of room to grow.

To determine how much floor (platform) space you need, try this: Clear out a corner of a room where

two walls meet at a right angle, then grab two tape measures. Pull out the tapes and lock them in place at any desired dimensions—for example, set both at 6 feet for a 36 square feet floor, or set one at 8 feet and one at 10 feet for an 80 square feet floor.

Lay the tapes on the floor so they meet at a right angle, representing the two imagined walls of your area. Step inside the area to get a feel for its size. Bring in some chairs and other furniture you might want in the treehouse to see how everything fits. Don't forget to factor in the tree, especially if you're building your platform around the trunk.

Not that your treehouse has to be square. In fact, this is a rare opportunity to build out of square. Why not a triangle or rhombus or something more amoeba-like? There are no points off for ignoring traditional design principles, like symmetry. You already have a house that follows the rules. When it comes to treehouses, quirks and funny angles add character and make it more personal.

USING POSTS

Treehouse snobs may balk at the use of support posts, but this is nothing to be ashamed of. Posts offer an effective way to compensate for trees that can't solely support a treehouse or for cases where a design calls for more trees than you have. Posts can also serve to shore up support beams with long spans between trees.

Keep in mind that using posts places limits on the house design. Namely, the house must be close to the ground. This is because the post will be cemented in the ground and essentially immovable, while the tree remains free to sway with the wind. In mature trees, movement typically is minimal in the lowest 10 to 12 percent of the tree's total height. Therefore, if you use posts as main support members, and the tree is 60 feet tall, for example, keep the platform within 6 to 7 feet of the ground.

STAY FLEXIBLE

As a final design tip, keep an open mind about changes. You might find yourself installing the walls when you discover that a window that was supposed to overlook the garden actually gives you a better view of the alley. Or, you might be surprised by the shadows within the canopy and decide to add an opening to bring in more sunlight. Building a treehouse is an organic process. Be ready to adapt.

Sturdy posts make strong treehouse supports, but are recommended only for treehouses with very little potential movement.

Drawing Plans

Spending a little time testing your ideas on paper almost always pays off when it comes time to build a treehouse. It's a lot easier to make changes to a few pencil lines than a lumber frame butted to a tree 10 feet in the air.

Start by taking some measurements of the building site; that is, the host trees. Measure the trunks, main branches, and relative positions of distinguishing marks and features. With those measurements and a little freehand sketching of the tree, you'll be able to make reasonably accurate scale drawings of the tree and treehouse from various perspectives.

Draw the platform first. Getting the platform right is the most challenging part of building a treehouse and usually requires some trial-and-error at the drawing board. If you don't want to make a complete set of plans, at least draw up the platform to test your ideas before you start building.

To experiment with ideas for the walls and roof, take a digital photo of the tree. Print it out at full-page size, then use your measurements of distinguishing features to get a sense of the photo's scale. Lay tracing paper over the photo to sketch your ideas. Take additional photos at different angles to the tree to create the various elevation drawings.

Elevation drawings show the house from various angles. These are helpful for judging proportions and planning for intervening branches, etc. Sketching over digital photo printouts gives you an accurate picture of how the finished project will look in the tree.

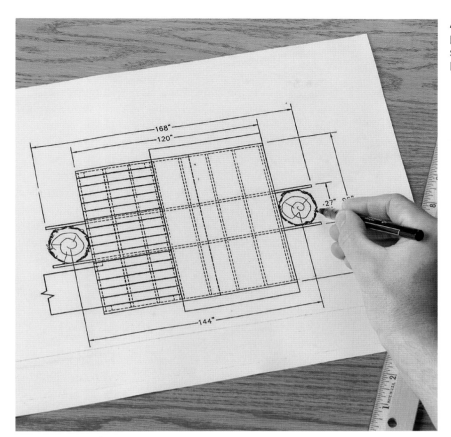

A floor plan showing the completed platform helps you divide up the floor space and allocate room for decks, landings, and other open areas.

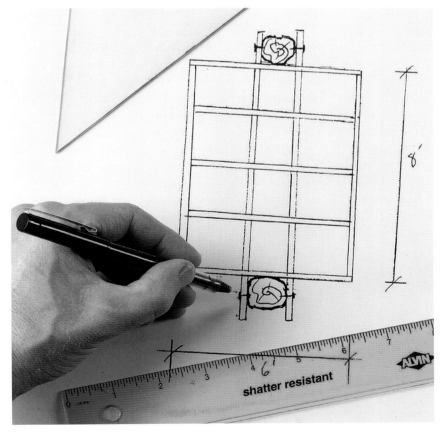

A plan view of the platform framing gives you a bird's-eye perspective of the host trees and main treehouse support members.

Lumber & Hardware

The classic kid-built treehouse is made with scrap wood, often "found" at a neighborhood construction site, and rusty nails fished out of a coffee can. Add some tar paper and carpet remnants, and you have yourself an awesome hideaway. It's still a great way to build a treehouse. But if that's what you had in mind, you probably wouldn't be reading this book (you'd be using it as a roof shingle). So what materials should you use on your next treehouse? The short answer is: everything rot-resistant and corrosion-resistant.

For lumber, the most commonly available types of rot-resistant wood are pressure-treated pine, cedar, and sometimes redwood. All of these can withstand years of weather without rotting. Even if your treehouse is kept dry with a sealed roof, it's a good idea to use one of these outdoor wood types on the interior parts as well, because you're bound to get some moisture inside.

Keep in mind that the reputations of cedar and redwood for rot-resistance really apply only to all-heartwood material, the higher quality lumber cut from the tree's hard center. Common-grade sapwood cedar and redwood aren't much more rot-resistant than standard untreated lumber. Also, cedar and redwood have lower load-bearing capacity than standard SPF and treated lumber, so be sure to check span ratings before using them for platform beams or other critical structural members.

If you use plywood in your project, choose the material based on how much it will be exposed to the elements: "Exterior" plywood is suitable for permanent exposure, while "Exposure 1" plywood is designed for outdoors but should be covered by other materials, such as roofing. Marine plywood is a premium plywood product designed for good looks and outdoor exposure. It's made with waterproof glue and won't delaminate with moisture, but the panels should be finished to prevent decay and discoloration of the wood.

For hardware, use hot-dipped or drop-forged galvanized steel—available in many types of bolts, screws, and connectors. Aluminum roofing nails are also acceptable. Stainless steel is the best and strongest rust-proof material but comes in a somewhat limited variety of hardware and costs a lot more than galvanized steel.

For any structural connections to the tree, use screws and bolts instead of nails. Bolts should be at least ½" in diameter and always galvanized for corrosion protection (or made of rust-proof material). Nails simply can't be trusted in trees. There's too much movement, and the live wood doesn't hold nails as consistently or predictably as dry lumber does. Galvanized nails are fine for framing connections and general construction of the house parts, although in many cases you might prefer to use deck screws or galvanized wood screws. With the smaller 2 × 2 and 2 × 3 framing used in treehouses, assembly is easier with screws.

Specialty connections and anchoring systems might call for Extra High Strength cable and high-tensile galvanized chain. Another hardware option available through a specialty supplier is the Garnier Limb (GL) treehouse anchor, which screws into the tree's trunk to serve as a heavy-duty limb for supporting platforms (see page 62).

RECLAIMED LUMBER & MATERIALS

Building a treehouse offers a great opportunity to scrounge around recycled lumber yards and architectural salvage shops for materials like weathered old timbers and one-of-a-kind fixtures. On top of being a fun scavenger hunt, this is also the best way to "build green." One note of caution, however: Inspect old lumber carefully before using it for structural members. Significant cracks, excessive knots, and evidence of rot are common indications that the wood might not be reliable or strong enough for its intended use.

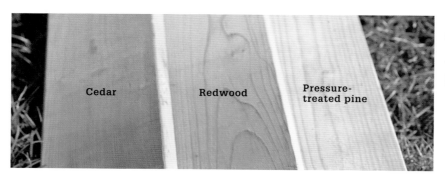

Lumber for treehouses must be suitable for outdoor exposure. This includes cedar, redwood, pressure-treated pine, and exterior-grade or marine plywood (not shown).

COMMONLY USED HARDWARE FOR TREEHOUSES

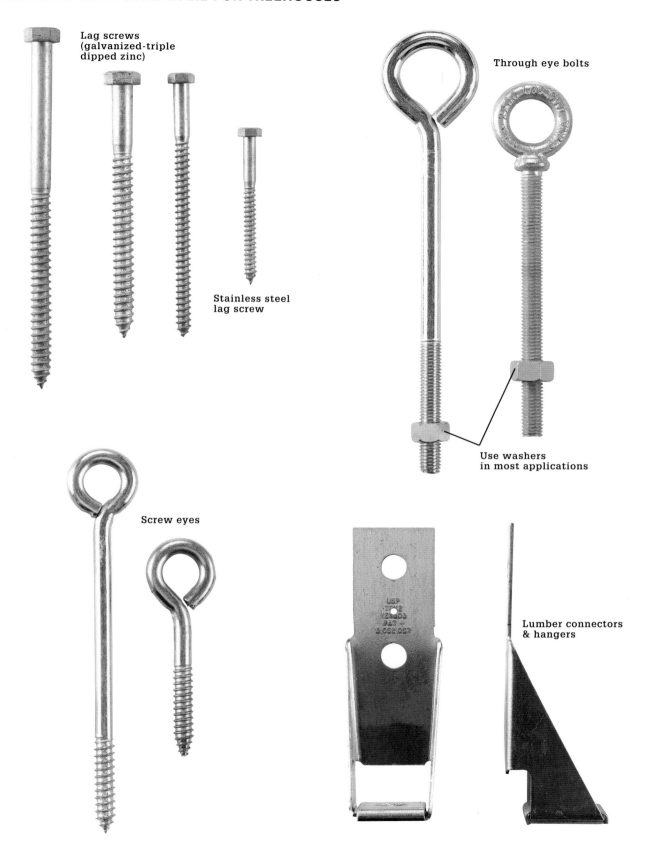

Lag screws
(galvanized-triple
dipped zinc)

Stainless steel
lag screw

Through eye bolts

Use washers
in most applications

Screw eyes

Lumber connectors
& hangers

MORE COMMONLY USED HARDWARE FOR TREEHOUSES

Galvanized nails and deck screws

Galvanized common nails

Coated deck screws

Galvanized high-tensile
chain (¾" link)

Galvanized washers

Pulley

Cable clamps and connectors

Wire rope thimble keeps wire rope from getting nicked

Wire rope clamp for securing a loop

A clevis is a type of fastener used to allow limited mobility to whatever is attached with the pin.

Quick link for joining chain links or fastening disparate parts together

EHS galvanized steel cable for suspending house elements and creating zip line runs

Treehouse Safety

A house up in a tree comes with some risks. But so does an elevated deck off of your kitchen or a jungle gym in your backyard. What makes you comfortable using these things on a daily basis is your belief that they were designed thoughtfully to prevent common hazards, combined with your own regular maintenance of the structures to ensure their safety. The same applies to treehouses, although treehouses present an additional safety consideration: building off the ground.

Therefore, treehouse safety can be divided into two categories: safe design and safe working conditions. Both are equally important and perfectly manageable, and both should be followed regardless of who uses the house. A kids' treehouse naturally involves more safety concerns than one used exclusively by adults. However, keep in mind that you never know when children might visit, and it's too late once they're up there. It's like bringing a two-year-old into a non-babyproofed home. The adults are suddenly scrambling madly as they discover all the things that are perfectly safe for them but potentially deadly for a toddler.

Safety is important during all phases of construction.

Safe Treehouse Design

The primary safeguard on any treehouse is the supporting platform. It alone keeps the house and its occupants aloft. Even if every other element is designed to the highest standards, a treehouse is completely unsafe if the platform isn't sound. A later chapter covers platform construction in detail, so for now, just two quick reminders:

1. Keep platforms for kids' treehouses at 8 feet above the ground or lower.
2. Inspect the platform support members and tree connections regularly to make sure everything's in good shape.

With a strong, stable platform in place, you can turn your attention to the other elements of safety in design.

Everything's riding on the treehouse platform. Be sure to keep it in good condition.

RAILINGS

Every part of a treehouse platform that isn't bound by walls must have a sturdy railing. Building codes around the country agree on railing specifications, and these are the best rules to follow for treehouses, too.

In general, railings must be at least 36" tall, with vertical balusters no more than 4" apart. A railing should be strong enough to withstand several adults leaning against it at once, as well as roughhousing kids. On treehouses for small children, use only standard 2 × 2 lumber or other rigid vertical balusters, not rope or cable balusters. For kids of all ages, don't use horizontal balusters. These work well for cattle fencing, but kids are too tempted to climb them. See page 93 for more railing specifications and instructions on building railings.

Sound, code-compliant railings are a critical safety feature for treehouse users of all ages.

A sturdy handle is a welcome sight to tired climbers. Make sure all handles and mounting hardware are galvanized or otherwise corrosion-protected.

ACCESS LANDINGS

Each type of access to a treehouse—ladder, rope, stairs, etc.—has its own design standards for safety, but all must have a landing point at which to arrive at or depart from the house. In many cases, the landing necessitates a gap in a railing or other opening and thus a potential fall hazard. Keep this in mind when planning access to your treehouse, and consider these recommendations:

- Include a safety rail across openings in railings.
- Leave plenty of room around access openings, enough for anyone to safely climb onto the treehouse platform and stand up without backing up.
- Consider non-slip decking on landings to prevent falls if the surface gets wet.
- Add handles at the sides of access openings and anywhere else to facilitate climbing up and down; handholds cut into the treehouse floor work well, too.
- Install a safety gate to bar young children from areas with access openings.

WINDOWS & DOORS

The obvious safety hazard for windows and doors is glass. So the rule is: Don't use it, especially in kids' treehouses. Standard glass is too easily broken during play or by swaying branches or rocks thrown by taunted older brothers. Instead, use strong plastic sheeting. The strongest stuff is ¼"-thick polycarbonate glazing. It's rated for outdoor public buildings, like kiosks and bus stops, so it can easily survive the abuse from your own little vandals. Plastic does get scratched and some becomes cloudy over time, but it's easily replaced and is better than a trip to the emergency room.

Even more important than the glazing is the placement of doors and windows. All doors and operable windows must open over a deck, not a drop to the ground. If a door is close to an access point, make sure there's ample floor space between the door and any opening in a railing, for example.

GROUND BELOW THE TREE

Since occasional short falls are likely to occur when kids are climbing around trees, it's a good idea to fill the area beneath your treehouse with a soft ground cover. The best material for the health of the tree is wood chips. A 6"-thick bed of wood chips effectively cushions a fall from 7 feet, according to the National Resource Center for Health and Safety in Child Care. Also, keep the general area beneath the house free of rocks, branches, and anything else one would prefer not to land on.

A soft bed of loose ground cover is recommended under any kids' treehouse or areas where kids will be climbing.

CONSTRUCTION DETAILS

One of the first rules of building children's play structures is to countersink all exposed hardware, and for good reason. If you fall and slide along a post, you might get a scrape and some splinters, but you're much better off than if your kneecap hits a protruding bolt on the way down. Follow the countersink rule for all kids' treehouses.

Speaking of splinters, take the time to sand rough edges as you build your house. Your kids and guests will be glad you did. Also keep an eye out for sharp points, protruding nails, and any rusty metal.

MAINTENANCE

Treehouses fight a constant battle with gravity. This, combined with outdoor exposure and the threat of rust and rot, make regular inspections of the house a critical safety precaution. Inspect your treehouse several times throughout the year for signs of rot or damage to structural members and all supporting hardware. Also check everything after big storms and high winds, as excessive tree movement can easily cause damage to wood structures or break anchors without you knowing it. Test safety railings, handholds, and access equipment more frequently.

Inspect the tree around connecting points for stress fractures and damage to the bark. Weighted members and tensioned cables and ropes rubbing against the bark can be deadly for a tree if they cut into the layers just below the bark. Check openings where the trunk and branches pass through the treehouse, and expand them as needed to avoid strangling the tree. Finally, remove dead or damaged branches that could fall on the house.

Neglected support beams and connections are the most common causes of treehouse disasters. Check these parts often for rot, corrosion, and damage.

Treefort Knox ▸

Locking up may seem unnecessary for most backyard hideaways, but for some treehouses it's a sensible precaution. For example, treehouses located out of your daily view, especially those near a public road, can attract a lot of negative attention, like vandalism. More important, kids just can't resist getting into stuff, and you don't want to face a lawsuit because you made it easy for them to waltz into your house and get hurt. Of course, you had nothing to do with it. But try telling that to a plaintiff lawyer.

These are just suggestions, not legal advice:

- Install a strong door with a padlock (¾" plywood backed by a lumber frame is a good choice; it may be ugly, but it's strong).
- Post signage stating "No Trespassing," "Private Property," "Danger," or similar warnings.
- Install window shutters that lock on the inside or can be padlocked from the outside.
- Use plastic instead of glass in windows (the polycarbonate glazing mentioned on page 53 won't be broken with rocks).

- Use a retractable or removable ladder as the only means of access, and take it away when you leave the treehouse.

Working Safely

Off-the-ground work has its own long list of safety guidelines on top of the regular set of basic construction safety rules. Since you can learn about general tool and job site safety anywhere (please do so), the focus here is on matters specific to treehouse building and related gravity-defying feats. But here are some good points to keep in mind.

During construction, ladder management is an exceptionally important aspect of jobsite safety. Since trees generally do not afford flat, smooth areas for the ladder rungs to rest, adding padded tips will help stabilize the ladder. And remember, a fall of just a couple of feet from a ladder can cause a fractured elbow or worse.

Working outdoors presents challenges not faced in the interior, such as dealing with the weather, working at heights, and staying clear of power lines. By taking a few common-sense safety precautions, you can perform exterior work safely.

Dress appropriately for the job and weather. Avoid working in extreme temperatures, hot or cold, and never work outdoors during a storm or high winds.

Work with a helper whenever possible—especially when working at heights. If you must work alone, tell a family member or friend so the person can check in with you periodically. If you own a portable phone, keep it with you at all times.

Don't use tools or work at heights after consuming alcohol. If you're taking medicine, read the label and follow the recommendations regarding the use of tools and equipment.

When using ladders, extend the top of the ladder three feet above the roof edge for greater stability. Climb on and off the ladder at a point as close to the ground as possible. Use caution and keep your center of gravity low when moving from a ladder onto a roof. Keep your hips between the side rails when reaching over the side of a ladder, and be careful not to extend yourself too far or it could throw off your balance. Move the ladder as often as necessary to avoid overreaching. Finally, don't exceed the work-load rating for your ladder. Read and follow the load limits and safety instructions listed on the label.

HARDHAT AREA (HEADS UP!)

The general area underneath the tree should be off limits to anyone not actively working on the project at hand. Someone walking idly underneath to check things out might not be engaged enough to react if something falls. Hard hats are a good idea for anyone working on the project and for kids anywhere close to the job site.

To keep an extension cord from dropping—and sometimes taking your tool with it—wrap the cord around a branch to carry the bulk of the weight. Also, wear a tool belt to keep tools and fasteners within reach while keeping your hands free to grab lumber or use tools.

PULLEY SYSTEMS

A pulley is one of the fun features found on a lot of treehouses. They're great for delivering baskets full of food and supplies. During the build, a simple pulley set up with a bucket or crate is handy for hauling up tools and hardware.

Here's an easy way to set up a simple, lightweight pulley:

1. Using a strong nylon or manila rope (don't use polypropylene, which doesn't stand up under sun exposure), tie one end to a small sandbag and throw it over a strong branch.
2. Tie a corrosion-resistant pulley near the end of the rope, then tie a loop closer to the end, using bowline knots for both (see below).
3. Feed a second rope through the pulley and temporarily secure both ends so the rope won't slip through the pulley.
4. Thread the first rope through the loop made in step 2, then haul the pulley up snug to the branch. Tie off the end you're holding to secure the pulley to the branch.

For heavy-duty lifting, use a block and tackle (see next page), which is a pulley system that has one rope strung through two sets of pulleys (blocks). The magic of multiple-pulley systems is that the lifting power is increased by 1× for each pulley. For example, a block and tackle with 6 pulleys gives you 6 pounds of lifting force for each pound of force you put onto the pulling rope. If you weigh 150 pounds and hang on the pulling end, you could raise a nearly 900-pound load without moving a muscle. The drawback is that you have to pull the rope 6× farther than if you were using a single pulley. For a high treehouse, you'll need a lot of rope.

When hauling up loads with a block and tackle, try to have a second person on the ground to man a control line tied to the load. This helps stabilize the load and steer it through branches and other obstacles. Additional control like this makes it safer for those up in the tree.

One rope raises and affixes the pulley to the tree; a second rope operates the pulley.

How to Tie a Bowline Knot ▶

Step 1: Make a loop in the rope so the working end (loose end) is on top of the standing portion of the rope.

Step 2: Run the working end up through the back of the loop, behind and around the standing rope, then down through the front of the loop.

Step 3: Tighten the knot by holding the working end in place while pulling up on the standing portion.

A block and tackle makes it easy to lift heavy support beams and pre-built walls.

Safety Checklist ▸

SAFE DESIGN CHECKLIST

❏ Platform no more than 8 feet above ground (for kids' treehouse).
❏ Strong railings 36" high, with balusters no more than 4" apart.
❏ Continuous railing along all open decks and at sides of stairs.
❏ Safety rail across all access openings.
❏ No horizontal railing balusters.
❏ Large access landings with handles or handholds as needed.
❏ No ladder rungs nailed to tree (see page 41).
❏ Non-slip decking around access openings.
❏ No glass windows in kids' treehouses.
❏ Doors and operable windows open onto a deck, not a drop.
❏ Soft ground cover beneath kids' treehouses.
❏ Hardware countersunk in all exposed areas.
❏ No rough wood edges, sharp points, or protruding nails or screws.
❏ Screws and bolts only for structural connections to tree; no nails (see page 46).
❏ Regular maintenance check of platform support members and tree connections, railings, access equipment, and handles.

SAFE CONSTRUCTION CHECKLIST

❏ Safety ropes and harness for any high work.
❏ Tie onto safety line even after platform is complete.
❏ No kids or visitors under tree during construction.
❏ Hardhats for workers on ground and all kids.
❏ Follow basic construction safety and ladder safety rules.
❏ No beer before quittin' time.

Treehouse Building Techniques

Building a treehouse is mostly an exercise in carpentry. But even if you have years of experience pounding nails and planing doors with your feet firmly on the ground, you'll find that everything changes once you're up in the air. The simplest tasks take on new challenges as you struggle to keep the counterforces of work from knocking you to the ground. But in the end, whether you're building a treehouse or an outhouse or a doghouse, the success of the project comes down to good design and sound techniques. We've discussed good design already. Now it's time to take a look at treehouse building techniques.

In this chapter:

- Building Platforms
- Platform Designs
- Framing & Finishing Walls
- Finishing Interiors
- Doors & Windows
- Building Roofs
- Modes of Access
- Swings & Playthings

Building Platforms

It's time to get this house off the ground. The platform is the first and most important part of the building process. It also tends to be the most challenging.

To build a proper platform, you'll need to determine what types of anchors will hold up best against the host tree's natural movement throughout the year. You'll also decide on sizing for support beams and floor framing, based on the size of your house and how much it will weigh (don't worry, you won't have to stand on a scale with each 2 × 4). As before, the tree should be your primary guide.

This chapter walks you through some basics of platform construction, the main types of anchors for support beams, and installation of the floor decking. You'll then get a construction overview of platforms for several popular treehouse configurations. Please keep in mind that all methods and configurations shown here are merely drawn from examples that have worked on other treehouses. On your own treehouse, you alone are the architect, engineer, and builder, and it's up to you to determine what is suitable for your situation. If you have any concerns about the structural viability of your platform or the health of your tree, consult a qualified building professional or arborist.

The treehouse platform needs to be solidly constructed, square, level, and (above all) securely attached to the tree or trees.

Platform Basics

A typical treehouse platform is made up of support beams and a floor frame. The beams are anchored to the tree and carry the weight of the entire structure. The frame is made up of floor joists that run perpendicular to the beams. Topped with decking, the floor frame becomes the finished floor of the treehouse, onto which you build the walls and everything thereafter. Some small kids' treehouses have only a floor as the supporting structure, particularly when the house is low to the ground and well supported by branches.

Sizing beams and floor joists isn't an exact science as it is with a regular house, but standard span tables can give you an idea about load limits for your treehouse. Contact your local building department for span tables and materials requirements for beams (also called girders), floor joists, and decking materials. What's unique to treehouses is the additional stress of the tree's motion and possible twisting forces applied to the floor frame. Flexible anchors are the best defense against tree motion, as you'll see later. In any case, it's better to err on the side of oversizing support members.

The trick to building a successful platform is not just in the strength and stability. The platform must also be level. If you've ever been in an old house with a sloping floor, you know why. It messes with your sense of equilibrium and gives you an uneasy "funhouse" feeling. In a treehouse this can lead to a perceived sense of instability; worse, it gives your friends and family something to make fun of. One handy technique for locating anchor points to create a level platform is to set up a mason's string and line level. A few more tips for building platforms:

- Use a single ¾"-diameter galvanized lag screw to anchor lumber directly to the tree. For lightweight supports, you can get away with ½" screws, but don't use anything smaller.
- If a situation calls for more than one screw in any part of the tree, never place two screws in a vertical line less than 12" apart. To the tree, each screw is treated as a wound; if the screws are too close together, the wounds might coalesce, causing the area to rot.
- Never remove bark to create a flat surface for anchoring, etc. If done carefully, it's okay to shave the surface slightly, but always leave the protective layer of bark intact. A better solution is to use wood wedges to level out brackets and other anchors.
- When you're building a platform up in the tree, it's often helpful to cut beams or joists long at first, allowing some play as you piece the frame together. Cut off the excess after the framing is completed, or leave beam ends long to use as outriggers for pulleys, swings, etc.

Fasteners placed close together in a vertical line can lead to rot in the tree, causing the anchors to fail.

Platform Anchoring Techniques

Anchoring the platform is all about dealing with tree movement. Here's the problem: If you're building in or around a section of the tree that's used to moving a lot in the wind and you tie multiple parts of the tree (or parts of different trees) together, something's got to give. Usually it's your platform's support beams or anchors that lose the battle by breaking or simply shearing off. The best solution is to respect Mother Nature by using anchors that make allowances for movement.

Treehouse builders have come up with a range of anchoring methods for different situations, but most fall into one of the four categories shown here. Knowing the main types of anchors will help you decide what's best for your project. Often a combination of different anchors is the most effective approach.

FIXED ANCHOR

A fixed anchor is the most basic type, with the support beams firmly anchored to the tree with large lag screws. Because they allow for zero tree movement, fixed anchors are typically used on single-tree houses anchored exclusively to the trunk, or perhaps used in conjunction with a flexible anchor (sliding or hanging—see below) at the opposite end of the beam.

To install a fixed anchor, drill a slightly oversized hole for a lag screw through the beam, just below the center of the beam's depth. Drill a pilot hole into the tree that's slightly smaller than the screw's shank. Add one washer on the outside of the beam and one or two large, thick washers on the tree side, and anchor the beam to the tree with the lag screw. The washers on the tree side of the beam help prevent chafing of the beam against the bark.

Sizing the screw: Use a ¾" galvanized lag screw that's long enough to penetrate at least 5" to 6" into the tree's solid wood. Accounting for a 2× (1½"-thick) beam, the washers, and the bark, you need at least a 9" screw for a major beam connection.

Centerline of beam

Centerline of screw hole

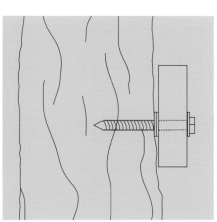

A single lag screw is an adequate fixed anchor for a beam, provided the screw is heavy enough. Multiple screws can cause damage to your tree. Thread a washer between the screw head and the beam, and add at least a couple washers between the beam and the tree to prevent the beam from rubbing against and damaging the bark.

SLIDING ANCHOR

There are two main types of sliding anchor: slot-type and bracket-type. The slot-type is a simple variation of the fixed anchor, but instead of drilling a hole in the beam for the lag screw, you cut a slot that allows for a few inches of lateral movement. This anchor is suitable for relatively small, low treehouses that don't warrant the heavy-duty support of a bracket-type connection. Using a ¾" lag screw and extra-large washers on both sides of the beam, make the slot 1" wide and 3" to 6" long. Leave the screw slightly loose to allow a little play for the beam to slide.

A bracket-type sliding anchor uses a metal bracket or cleat mounted to the tree to support the beam from below. As the tree moves, the beam is free to slide along the top of the support without rubbing against the tree. A properly engineered and installed bracket makes a very strong anchor suitable for large treehouses.

Unfortunately, they don't sell treehouse brackets at your local hardware store. So how do you get

them? One way is to have them custom built to your specifications by a qualified welder. Another option is to use the Garnier Limb (see page 46), a manufactured metal anchor specifically designed for supporting treehouse beams. The GL has a threaded screw end that screws into the tree and a smooth "limb" end that supports the beam.

The developers of the GL have come up with many variations based on their basic anchor to accommodate various treehouse configurations. You can see the GL in action and get ordering and installation information on their website: www.treehouses.com. According to the website, the basic installation of a GL has a load rating of 4,000 pounds.

HANGING ANCHOR

With a hanging anchor, the beams are actually suspended from the tree by cables or moveable hardware, making it the most flexible type of joint. This flexibility makes it ideal for difficult applications,

A slot-type sliding anchor allows single-directional movement between the tree or trees and the platform beams.

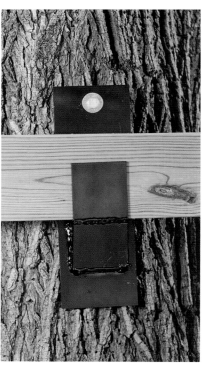

A bracket-type sliding anchor allows two-directional movement while offering solid support. Unfortunately, you'll have to have these custom-fabricated at a local metal shop.

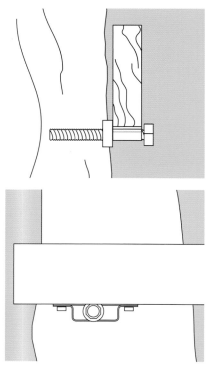

A specialty treehouse anchor offers the best combination of strength and movement allowance. The GL anchor illustrated here is very popular with professional treehouse builders and can be purchased on the Internet (see Resources, page 220).

A hanging anchor with cable attaches to a screw eye in the tree and a doubled ¾" chain wrapped around the beam.

Through eye bolts

Shackle

Nut and bearing plate

A through bolt hanging anchor requires a tree limb at least 6" in diameter.

such as when tree movement is significant or when the branch or trunk configuration won't easily accommodate a platform. *Note: The minimum branch size for hanging anchors (at the connection point) is 6" diameter, depending on the tree and treehouse.*

As with the sliding anchor, there are different styles of hanging connections. A basic cable setup offers the best flexibility: Cut a 6-foot length of heavy-duty rust-proof cable, then cut enough high-tensile rust-proof chain to wrap around the beam twice, plus a few extra links. Drive a ⅝" eye lag screw into the tree, about 4 feet above the desired beam elevation. Position the eye screw so its shaft will be perpendicular to the cable when hung. This ensures that the load will rely more on the screw's shear strength than the grip of the threads.

Hang the beam in the tree at the desired elevation, using temporary lines. Thread the cable through the eye screw, using a cable thimble to protect the cable, then secure the end with three cable clamps. Wrap the beam with the chain and

secure the ends to the cable, again using a thimble and three clamps. To prevent the beam from slipping out of the anchor, make sure plenty of beam extends past the chain, and install a strong metal bracket that loosely captures the chain at the bottom edge of the beam.

Another type of hanging anchor uses a long, ⅝" eye through bolt that extends completely through a support branch. At the other end, another eye bolt extends through the beam and is secured below. The two eyes are connected with a heavy-duty shackle, allowing some movement in all directions.

Bolting through the branch won't hurt the tree, but the branch must be at least 6" in diameter for this application. Make sure to use a strong washer on the top side of the branch, as well as a washer or steel bearing plate below the beam. If you use a built-up beam (with two 2× boards nailed together), add pairs of carriage bolts along both sides of the eye bolt to keep the beam members together when the anchor is under stress.

Knee braces support the platform, distributing the load onto the trunk and off of the lag screws that attach the beams to the tree trunk.

With any type of hanging anchor, it's important that the beam and cable or hardware do not rub against the tree. If your setup doesn't allow for at least 6" of play between the beam/hanger and the tree, fasten a wood block to the tree to protect against chafing that could damage the bark and underlying layers. Also, never hang a support cable or chain by running it over a branch or wrapping it around a branch or trunk. This can kill part or all of the tree.

KNEE BRACES

Knee braces help support many types of platforms after the main beams have been attached to the tree. As such, they might be considered secondary anchors but nevertheless are critical to many platform designs.

A knee brace essentially is an angled strut that forms a structural triangle with the platform and tree. It is strongest when set at 45° (or as close as possible to that angle). There are numerous designs of braces for treehouses, but all follow the same principle of the triangle.

For strength, the top end of the brace should meet the beam or frame at least ⅔ of its total distance from the tree. Don't worry if the braces aren't all the same length; it's more important to maintain the 45° angle. To join the top end of the brace to the corner of a platform frame, use adjustable framing connectors. To anchor to the underside of a beam or joist, use pairs of metal joining plates, bolted to both members with carriage bolts.

Attaching the brace to the tree is another matter. Large, professionally built (yes, there are people who get to do this for a living) treehouses often use custom metal brackets to affix knee braces to the tree. An easy amateur method is to use an adjustable framing connector screwed to the tree and fastened to the brace with nails.

Installing Decking

If you're thinking that you've just jumped from platform beams to decking and skipped the floor framing, you're right. Because the configuration of the floor framing tends to follow the platform design, you'll get a better picture of that with the individual construction overviews starting on page 66.

Most treehouse platforms are decked using standard decking techniques. It's a lot like decking a...well, a deck, or a floor, depending on the materials used. Standard decking materials include 5/4 × 6 decking boards, 2 × 6 lumber, and ¾" exterior-grade plywood. Of these, plywood is the cheapest and easiest to install, but it comes with one drawback: treehouse floors tend to get wet, and the water has no place to go on a solid plywood surface. By contrast, decking boards can—and should—be gapped to allow water through and eliminate pooling. If you're really committed to creating a dry interior on your house,

you might consider plywood or tongue & groove decking boards, which make a smooth, strong floor without gaps.

Install decking boards with deck screws driven through pilot holes (although you would normally nail T&G boards). Use screws that are long enough to penetrate the floor framing by at least 1¼". Gap the boards ¼" apart, or more, if desired. Two screws at each joist are sufficient. Install plywood decking with 2" deck screws, driven every 6" along the perimeter and every 8" in the field of the sheet.

To allow for tree growth, try to leave a 2" gap between the decking and the tree. This means you'll have to scribe the decking and cut it to fit around tree penetrations. To scribe a board, set it on the floor as close as possible to its final position, then use a compass to trace the contours of the tree onto the board.

Fasten the decking to the floor frame with corrosion-resistant deck screws. Use a compass (right) to scribe decking boards at tree penetrations.

2" gap

Platform Designs

Following are five examples of platforms in different tree configurations, along with construction overviews for building the platforms as shown. Hopefully they will help you generate ideas for building your own platform. These examples are for demonstration purposes only. The proper sizing of support beams, joists, and hardware, as well as platform configuration, must be based on your tree and house project.

A **single-tree treehouse** often is constructed so the tree penetrates the platform more or less in the middle. The platform is supported by beams that are lag-screwed to the tree. This platform will be reinforced with knee braces.

Single Tree: Platform Nestled in Branches

This is a simple platform design suitable for a small kids' treehouse. Because the platform is small (about 5 × 6 feet) and has support from several branches, there are no support beams. Instead, a sturdy floor frame made with 2 × 6s is anchored directly to the tree. To account for slight branch movement, two of the four anchors are slot-type sliding connections and two are fixed anchors. The floor decking is ¾" plywood. For this type of platform, the support branches should be at least 6" in diameter.

FINDING THE ANCHOR POINTS

Using four nails and a mason's string, plot the rough platform shape onto the support branches. Attach a line level to the string, and work your way around the four sides, adjusting the nails up or down as needed to create a level layout. Each nail represents an anchor point, as well as the approximate center of the floor frame members. When you're satisfied with the layout, remove the string, but leave the nails in place to help with measuring and positioning the frame members.

INSTALLING THE RIM JOISTS

Using the nails for reference, measure the approximate length of the first rim joist. Cut the joist long by about 12" to allow for some play when positioning the two perpendicular rim joists. Mark the locations of the two fixed anchor points onto the board, then drill a through hole for a ¾" lag screw, a little below the center of the board's depth

(see page 61). Reposition the joist in the tree, then check it for level. Drill a ⅝"-diameter pilot hole into the tree at one of the anchor points. Add washers to both sides of the joist, and fasten the joist with a lag screw. Holding the joist level, drill a pilot hole and install the second fixed anchor.

Tip: If the joist won't install plumb because the branch is not vertical, glue a wood wedge behind the joist with construction adhesive.

Cut the two rim joists that run perpendicular to the first rim joist. Have a helper hold one end while you level and mark the anchor point on the other end. Cut a 1 × 3" to 1 × 6" slot for the sliding anchor, and fasten the joist to the tree with a lag screw and washers (see page 62). Then, endnail the joists together with 16d galvanized common nails. Install the opposing joist and fasten it to the first rim joist. Cut the fourth rim joist to fit and fasten it with endnails. Cut off the long ends of the first rim joist so they're flush with the mating joists.

Use a mason's line and line level to find at least four level anchor points for the platform.

Anchor one end of the rim joist, then level the joist and anchor the other end. Glue a custom-cut wedge (right) between the joist and the tree.

Cut the common joists to fit and tack them in place with deck screws so the tops are level. Then drive three 16d nails at each joint (nails have much greater shear strength than screws).

ADDING THE COMMON JOISTS

Mark the common joist layout onto the two long rim joists so they will run parallel to the short sides of the frame. Space the joists at 16" or 24" on center; either spacing is strong enough for a small treehouse. Cut the 2 × 6 joists to fit and install them with three 16d galvanized nails at each end.

INSTALLING THE DECKING

Cut the ¾" exterior-grade plywood decking to fit so any seams fall on the center of a common joist. Fasten the decking to the joists with 2" deck screws.

Single Tree: Trunk as Center Post

A tall, straight trunk is the foundation for this platform design that measures 8 feet square. It starts with two intersecting sets of 2 × 8 beams stacked on top of each other. All beams are fastened to the tree with a single fixed anchor screw. The upper two beams become floor joists in the finished frame. Each corner of the frame is supported by a knee brace, transferring much of the load back down to the tree trunk. The braces are fastened to the frame and tree with galvanized metal framing connectors. The decking is 5/4 × 6 boards, which saves a little on weight compared to 2 × 6 decking. The tree for this type of platform should measure at least 5 feet in circumference at its base.

Note: The platform frame is not safe to stand on before the knee braces are installed.

Diagram labels: 8', 8', 2 × 8 knee brace below, Trunk, 2 × 8 upper beam, 2 × 8 lower beam, 2 × 8 common joists, 2 × 8 rim joists

A single-trunk treehouse will accomodate most designs for small to medium size treehouses.

How to Build a Single-tree Platform

Measure to find locations of platform and bracing, and mark them on the tree with colored tape.

Drill into the tree to make pilot holes for the lag screws. Because you will be driving only one screw per beam, you can thread the screw through a guide hole in the beam with washers on both sides of the beam, then insert the screw tip into the pilot hole in the tree.

INSTALLING THE BEAMS

Cut the lower 2 × 8 beams at 96", and cut the upper 2 × 8 beams at 93". If possible, find a relatively flat, smooth area of the tree trunk to install the beams. Anchor the first lower beam to the tree with a lag screw, centering the screw along the board's length and on the tree's trunk. Install the second lower beam on the opposite side of the trunk, making sure the two beams are level with each other and are even on the ends. Install the

upper beams on top of the lower beams, following the same procedure.

ADDING THE RIM JOISTS

Cut two 2 × 8 side rim joists at 96" and two end rim joists at 93". The end joists are parallel to the upper beams. Fasten the side joists over the ends of the end joists, using three 16d common nails at each joint. Check the frame for square, then toenail the rim joists to both sets of beams.

(continued)

Secure the lower support beam to the tree trunk using a large socket wrench. Check for level as you tighten the bolt.

Level the second lower support beam of the platform base, making sure it is parallel with the first.

Use shims as needed to help any beams stand plumb where the tree surface is not vertical.

6

Make sure the beams are level with each other before anchoring them to the trunk.

INSTALLING THE KNEE BRACES

Cut each 2 × 8 knee brace to length so it extends at a 45° angle from one of the inside corners of the rim joist frame to the tree trunk; miter the ends of the braces at 45°. Install an adjustable framing connector (typically used for rafters) at each corner of the frame to secure the top end of each brace. Install a bracket to the tree for the bottom end of each brace. Then, install the braces.

Note: For a large or heavy treehouse, you might need to use two 2 × 8s or a 4 × 6 or larger timber for each knee brace to ensure adequate support.

COMPLETING THE FLOOR FRAME

Cut two 2 × 6 common joists to fit between the side rim joists and install them midway between the upper beams and the end rim joists. Install two short joists that span from the side rim joists to the trunk. Install these midway between the upper beams.

DECKING THE PLATFORM

Install the 5/4 × 6 decking boards perpendicular to the common joists, keeping the decking flush with the outsides of the floor frame. Gap the boards by ¼" and fasten them to the rim joists, common joists, and upper beams with 2½" deck screws.

(continued)

7

Framing connectors make for strong joints at both ends of the knee braces.

8

Toenail all of the joists to the lower beams with 16d galvanized common nails.

Two Trees: Platform Spanning Between Trunks

Two large trees spaced about 6 feet to 8 feet apart allow for an open platform with a simple structure. This platform is supported by two 2 × 10 beams attached on both sides of the host trees with fixed anchors. The floor frame cantilevers to the sides of the beams and must be supported at each corner with a 2 × 6 knee brace anchored to the side of the tree. This rigid design is suitable for mature trees (at least 10" in diameter) at a low height where movement is slight. As shown, the platform decking is made of 2 × 6 boards. Thinner decking boards require two additional common joists to reduce the joist spacing to about 16" on center.

Note: The platform frame is not safe to stand on before the knee braces are installed.

Two-trunk treehouse platforms require more planning and engineering but can support a larger structure.

INSTALLING THE BEAMS

Cut the two 2 × 10 beams to extend several inches beyond the trees at both ends. Anchor one end of the first beam using a ¾" lag screw and washers. Hold the beam perfectly level, then anchor the other end to the other tree. Install the second beam on the opposite sides of the trees, making sure the beam is level and that both beams are level with each other.

BUILDING THE FLOOR FRAME

You can build the entire floor frame on the ground, then install it on top of the beams. Just make sure the frame will fit between the trees before completing the frame. Cut the two 2 × 8 end rim joists at 72" and the two side rim joists at 93". Cut the three 2 × 8 common joists at 69".

Nail the end rim joists over the ends of the side rim joists with three 16d common nails per joint so the joists are flush at their top edges. Space the common joists evenly between the end joists, and fasten them to the side joists with 16d nails.

Center the frame on top of the platform beams. Check the frame for square, then toenail the common joists and end rim joists to the beams.

INSTALLING THE KNEE BRACES

Each 2 × 6 knee brace starts about 3" in from the end of the end rim joist and extends down to the center of the tree trunk at a 45° angle. Cut each brace so its top end is flush with the bottom edge of the rim joist (or you can fit the brace into a notch in the joist, as shown below) and its bottom end has a plumb cut at 45°. Attach the braces to the rim joists with pairs of galvanized metal jointing plates and carriage bolts (see below). Anchor the bottom end of each brace to the tree with a ¾" lag screw and washers.

DECKING THE PLATFORM

Cut the 2 × 6 decking boards at 96" to run parallel to the side rim joists. Space the boards ¼" apart and fasten them to the floor joists with 3" deck screws, keeping all edges flush to the outsides of the floor frame.

Secure the braces to the floor frame with metal plates and carriage bolts. Anchor the braces to the tree with lag screws (right).

Install each beam so it is level and both beams are level with each other.

Build the 2 × 8 joist frame on the ground, then lift it up onto the platform beams.

Three Trees: Platform Spanning Between Trunks

With the strength of three large trees and heavy-duty bracket-type anchors, this platform is ready for a large, one-story treehouse. The main supports are three 4 × 12 beams, each anchored to a pair of tree trunks.

The platform floor frame is built with 2 × 10 joists spaced 16" on center. It cantilevers about 18" over the front beam, creating a nice spot for a deck area. For decking, the front third of the platform will be laid with 5/4 × 6 decking lumber, while the rear two-thirds will be decked with ¾" exterior-grade plywood in the area where the treehouse will sit.

Use the three-trunk platform for spaceships, pirate ships, and other larger-than-life treehouse ideas.

INSTALLING THE BRACKETS & BEAMS

Cut the 4 × 12 beams to length so they will overhang the mounting brackets by at least 12" at each end. Working on one beam at a time, mark the positions for the brackets onto the tree trunks. *Note: If you're installing a GL (see page 62), you'll need a specially sized bit available for purchase or rent through the GL supplier. Using the bit, drill a pilot hole into the trunk so that the GL will be perfectly level when installed. Drive the threaded end of the GL into the pilot hole, using a large pipe wrench, until the flange is firmly seated against the tree.*

Install the brackets and beams one at a time to make sure each beam is level and all beams are level with one another. With a GL system, install a GL floating bracket at each anchor point, following the manufacturer's instructions. Also install a stopper nut on the end of each GL to prevent the beam from slipping off the GL.

BUILDING THE FLOOR FRAME

Cut the two 2 × 10 end rim joists to length so they fit between the two front trees with a few inches of play at each end (108" in this example). Cut the two side rim joists and six common joists at 117". On the end rim joists, mark the layout of the common joists, using 16" on-center spacing. Assemble the rim joist frame on top of the beams, using 16d common nails. Measure the diagonals to make sure the frame is square, then install the common joists.

When the common joists aren't supported by a side beam at the rear of the floor frame, reinforce the joists with joist hangers where they meet the rear end rim joist. Check the frame again for squareness, then toenail all of the joists to the beams with pairs of 16d galvanized nails.

DECKING THE PLATFORM

Snap a chalkline across the joists to represent the outside edge of the treehouse's wall framing. Install 5/4 × 6 decking boards perpendicular to the common joists, starting at the front edge of the floor frame and stopping at the chalk line. Fasten the boards with 2½" deck screws. Install ¾" exterior-grade plywood from the edge of the decking to the rear edge of the floor frame, using 2" deck screws.

Add joist hangers to the longest-spanning joists to strengthen their connection to the rear rim joist.

Two Trees & Two Support Posts

Four trees forming a perfect square or rectangle makes for an easy treehouse foundation, but this just doesn't occur often in nature. The platform design shown here provides the same layout with only two trees, and it takes care of tree movement with a floor frame that slides along the top of a support beam. The two posts are 4 × 4 or 6 × 6 timbers buried in the ground, set in concrete and reinforced laterally with knee braces. The posts and 2 × 10 floor frame create a very rigid structure, while the 4 × 12 beam has the freedom to move on two sliding anchors (see page 62). Using 2 × 6 boards for decking helps to strengthen the floor frame. For a moderately sized treehouse, the trees for this platform design should be at least 10" in diameter.

A support-post design makes building a treehouse possible on sites with extreme slopes or where trees are scarce or do not lend themselves to your preferred configuration.

SETTING THE POSTS

Mark the post locations on the ground, allowing for several inches of play between the trees. Dig the post holes 14" in diameter and down to a depth below the frost line (check with the local building department for post-depth requirements in your area), plus 4". Fill the holes with 4" of compactible gravel for drainage.

Cut the posts long, then trim them to the platform height after the frame is installed. Set the posts in their holes and secure them with temporary cross bracing so they are perfectly plumb and are square to the platform layout. Fill the holes with concrete and let it dry.

INSTALLING THE SUPPORT BEAM

Cut the 4 × 12 beam to extend at least 12" beyond the tree anchor points at each end. Transfer level over from the posts with a mason's string and line level, and mark the post height onto the trees; measure down 9¼" (or the depth of the floor frame, if not 9¼") from these marks to determine the top of the support beam. Install the beam using support hardware at each end.

BUILDING THE FLOOR FRAME

Cut the two 2 × 10 end rim joists at 96". Cut the two side rim joists and five common joists at 117". Install the side rim joists and one end rim joist flush with the tops of the post, using pairs of ½" lag screws. Fasten the other end rim joist over the ends of the side joists with 16d common nails. Install the common joists using 16" on-center spacing, fastening them to the end rim joists with joist hangers.

ADDING THE KNEE BRACES

Cut the four 2 × 6 knee braces at 48", mitering the ends at 45° to fit flush to the rim joists and post corners, respectively. Fasten the braces to the side/end rim joists using galvanized metal joining plates and carriage bolts. Fasten the bottom ends of the braces to the outsides of the posts with pairs of ½" lag bolts or carriage bolts.

DECKING THE PLATFORM

Measure the diagonals of the floor frame to make sure it's perfectly square. Install 2 × 6 decking perpendicular to the common joists, using 2½" deck screws. Space the boards ¼" apart.

Secure the posts with cross bracing, then anchor them in place with concrete.

Install the common joists with joist hangers using the manufacturer's recommended fasteners.

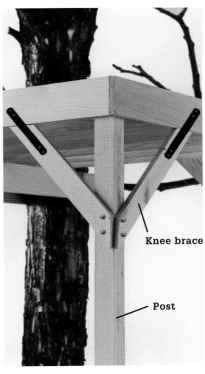

Knee brace

Post

Secure the knee braces to the outsides of the posts with ½" lag screws and metal straps.

Framing & Finishing Walls

With the platform done, you're now free to cut loose with your fine carpentry and creative design skills . . . well, you can use them if you have them. If not, it's ok. The point is, treehouse walls are fun and easy to build, and your new house will start to take shape before you know it. And because much of wall building is relatively lightweight work, it's also a good time to get the kids more involved, for those lucky enough to have some helping hands.

When building a regular house, carpenters frame the walls on the platform, then tip them into place and fasten them to the floor. That can be difficult in a treehouse; instead frame the walls on a driveway or other flat spot. In most cases, you can add the siding,

windows, and doors, and even the exterior trim, before sending the whole shebang up into the air. Assemble the completed wall panels with some screws, and presto! you have a house (a topless house, at least; roofs are covered in the next chapter).

Before you get started with the wall framing, plan all the steps of the wall building process—framing, siding, trim, and building windows and doors—to establish the best order of things for your project. If you're using plywood siding, for example, you'll add the siding before the windows, doors, and trim. Other types of siding go on after everything else. In any case, the sequence of information given here should not be interpreted as a specific order to follow.

Once the walls of your treehouse begin to take shape the excitement over your castle in the clouds will build tremendously.

Framing Walls

In the interest of making friends with gravity, treehouse walls are typically framed with 2 × 2 or 2 × 3 lumber, as opposed to the standard 2 × 4 or 2 × 6 framing used in traditional houses. Single-story treehouses can usually get away with 24" on-center stud spacing instead of the standard 16" spacing. However, the siding you use may determine the spacing, as some siding requires support every 16".

How tall you build the walls is up to you. Standard wall height is 8 feet. Treehouses have no standard, of course, but 6 feet to 7 feet gives most people enough headroom while maintaining a more intimate scale appropriate for a hideaway. Another consideration is wall shape. Often two of the four walls follow the shape of the roof, while the two adjacent walls are level across the top. Building wall shapes other than the rectangle or square are discussed later.

BASIC WALL CONSTRUCTION

A wall frame has horizontal top and bottom plates fastened over the ends of vertical studs. Where a window is present, a horizontal sill and header are installed between two studs to create a rough opening (door rough openings have only a header, along the top). On treehouses, similar framed openings can be used to frame around large tree penetrations.

In a four-walled structure, two of the walls are known as "through" walls and two are "butt" walls. The only difference is that through walls overlap the ends of the butt walls and are made longer to compensate for the thickness of the butt walls. For simplicity, the two through walls and two butt walls oppose each other so that both members of each type are made the same length.

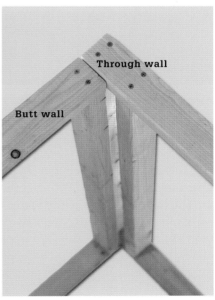

Build stud walls on the ground and then lift them up onto the platform one wall at a time. Through walls overlap butt walls (right) and are fastened together to form a corner of the house.

Assemble the wall frame with screws or nails. Add short cripple studs to continue the general stud layout at window and door openings.

To build a wall frame, cut the top and bottom plates to equal the total wall length (not counting the siding and trim). Lay the plates together on the ground—or driveway or garage floor—with their ends even. Mark the stud layout onto the plates, using 16" or 24" on-center spacing. Mark for an extra stud at each side of window and door openings; these are in addition to, and should not interrupt, the general stud layout. If you plan to install interior paneling or other finish, add an extra end stud to each end of the through walls. This gives you something to nail to when the walls are fitted together. Extra studs might also come in handy for nailing exterior siding.

Cut the studs to equal the total wall height minus 3", the combined thickness of the plates. Position the plates over the ends of the studs, and fasten them with two 3" galvanized wood screws or deck screws driven through pilot holes. You can screw through the plates into the ends of the studs, or angle the screws

(toenail) through opposing sides of the studs and into the plates. You can also use 10d or 16d galvanized nails instead of screws.

To frame a window opening, measure up from the bottom of the bottom plate and mark the sill and header heights onto both side studs. *Note: If you're using a homemade window, make the rough opening 1½" wider and 2¼" taller than the finished (glazed) window dimensions. This accounts for the window jambs made from ¾"-thick lumber and a sill made from 2 × 4 lumber. If you're using a recycled window sash (without its own frame), make the rough opening 1¾" wider and 2½" taller than the sash. Cut the sill and header and install them between the side studs, making sure the rough opening is perfectly square. Install short cripple studs below the sill and above the header to complete the general stud layout. Follow the same procedure to frame a rough opening for a door, making it 2½" wider and 1¼" taller than the finished door opening (for a homemade door).*

FRAMING OTHER WALL SHAPES

If you're going with a gable or shed roof for your treehouse, frame the two end walls to follow the roof slope. This not only encloses the walls up to the roof, it also establishes the roofline so you have an easy starting point for framing the roof. Houses with hip roofs have four standard walls—with horizontal top plates. Curved walls (for conical roofs) are also flat across the top but are framed a little differently than standard walls.

To frame an end wall for a gable or shed roof, first determine the roof's slope. In builders' parlance, roof slope, or pitch, is expressed in a rise-run ratio. For example, a 6-in-12 roof rises 6" for every 12" of horizontal run, equivalent to an angle of about 26.5°. A 12-in-12 roof slopes at 45°. For most do-it-yourselfers, it's easier to determine the roof slope using only the angle. Another trick to simplify roof framing is to lay out the entire outline of the wall by snapping chalk lines onto a garage floor or mat of plywood sheets. Then you can simply measure to your lines to find the lengths of the pieces.

For a gable end wall, let's say the roof slope is 30° (that's a little flatter than a 7-in-12 pitch). That means the top ends of all the studs, as well as the top ends of the two top plates, are cut at 30°. Snap a chalk line to represent the bottom of the wall, then snap two lines perpendicular to the first, representing the ends of the wall. *Note: The gable end wall must be a through wall.*

Measure up from the bottom line and mark the side lines at the total wall height; this is equal to the total height of the side (non-sloping) walls.

Now make a center line running up through the middle of the wall layout. Cut one end of each of the two top plates at 30°, leaving the other ends long for now. Set the angled ends of the plates together so they meet on the center line and each plate also intersects one of the top-of-wall marks on a side line. See your wall now? You can trace along the undersides of the top plates, or just leave them in place, then measure up from the bottom line to find the lengths of all the studs. Remember to take off 1½" from the stud lengths to account for the bottom plate. Cut the top plates to length so their bottom ends will be flush with the outside faces of the side walls.

To lay out an end wall for a shed roof—let's say at 15°—snap a bottom chalk line and two perpendicular side lines, as with the gable end wall. The end walls for a shed roof must also be through walls. Mark the wall heights onto the side lines. Snap a chalk line between those two marks, and your layout is done. All of the top ends of the studs are cut at 15°.

Shed end wall layout with 15° roof pitch.

Gable end wall layout with 30° roof pitch.

FRAMING CURVED WALLS

Structurally, curved walls are essentially the same as standard walls. They have top and bottom plates, studs, and similar rough openings for windows and doors. The main difference, and the trick to making the curve, is in using a double layer of ¾" plywood for each of the plates. Also, the stud spacing is set according to the exterior siding material. Use 2 × 3 or larger studs for framing curved walls.

Lay out curved wall plates using a trammel: a thin, flat board with a pivot nail near one end and two holes for a pencil near the other end. Space the pencil holes to match the width (depth) of the wall's studs. The distances between the pencil holes and the pivot nail determine the inner and outer radii of the curve. Mark the plate outlines onto full or partial sheets of ¾" exterior-grade plywood, and make the cuts with a jigsaw (or circular saw for gentle curves). You can piece together the plates as needed to minimize waste.

Space the studs according to the siding you'll use: For plywood, space the studs 2" for every 12" of outside radius on the curve—a 36" radius gets studs every 6". For other types of siding, such as vertical 1 × 4 T&G boards, lay out the studs at 24" on center, then install 2× nailers horizontally between the studs along the midpoint of the wall. The nailers must be cut with the same radius as the wall plates.

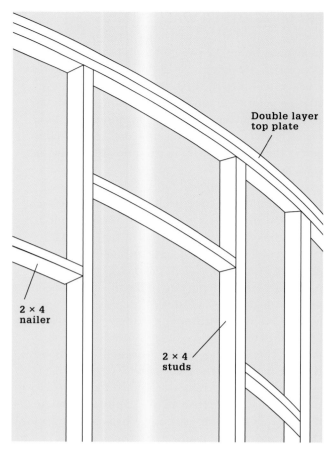

Double layer top plate

2 × 4 nailer

2 × 4 studs

Install 2× nailers between studs for vertical siding. Stagger the nailers up and down to allow room for fastening.

Use a trammel to mark the cutting lines for curved wall plates, pivoting the trammel from a centerline.

Siding & Trim

Most standard types of house siding are suitable for a treehouse. You might want to match the siding on your regular house or go with something unconventional, such as corrugated metal. Just try to keep the overall weight in check. For that reason, heavy material like hardboard siding isn't a great choice. Three of the most popular types of siding are shown here.

Note: Always make sure your wall frame is square before installing siding or trim.

PLYWOOD SIDING

Available in a variety of styles, in 4 × 8-foot panels and thicknesses from ⅜" to ⅝", plywood siding is quick and easy to install, and it adds a lot of strength to walls. It is somewhat heavy though, so you should use the thinnest material that's appropriate. For regular houses, ⅜" plywood siding can be used over studs spaced 16" on center, while ½" or thicker is recommended for 24" stud spacing. On a treehouse, ⅜" is usually fine for either spacing, but it's up to you. Trim goes on after the plywood siding.

Install plywood siding vertically, so the panels meet over the centers of the wall studs. Many types of siding have special edges that overlap at the joints to keep out water; join these according to the manufacturer's instructions. If the panel edges are square, leave a ⅛" gap at the joint, and fill the gaps with caulk after installation. Fasten the panels to the wall framing with galvanized box or siding nails. Nail every 6" along the perimeter and every 12" in the field of the panel.

On through walls, wrap the wall ends with a narrow strip of siding. On butt walls, stop the siding flush with the ends of the walls.

Use the square factory edges of plywood siding panels to square-up the wall frame. Fasten along one edge of the panel, then align the framing and fasten along the adjacent panel edge.

Common Siding Joints ▶

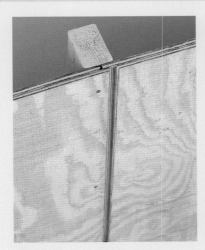  

Three common siding joints include shiplap edges (left photo) or other milled profiles that allow overlapping of panels; butt joints (center photo), where square-edged panels are gapped at about ⅛" and sealed with caulk; and board and batten joints (right photo), which get a 1 × 2 strip covering the panel gaps (battens are nailed to wall studs).

HORIZONTAL (LAP) SIDING

Classic cedar lap siding is an attractive, lightweight material. It takes more time to install than plywood, and it's more expensive, but it definitely adds charm to a treehouse. Most lap siding requires studs spaced 16" on center. It's easiest to install after the trim. *Note: For a large or multi-story treehouse, you might need a base layer of plywood sheathing underneath lap siding, to give the wall sufficient shear strength; consult your local building department or a qualified building professional.*

To install lap siding, cut the boards one at a time so they fit snugly between the vertical trim boards. Begin with a starter strip at the bottom of the wall, then work your way up, overlapping each preceding course by at least 1". Nail into each stud with galvanized box nails or siding nails, driving the nails just above the top edge of the siding board below. You may have to add studs near the ends of walls to provide a nailing surface for the ends of the siding.

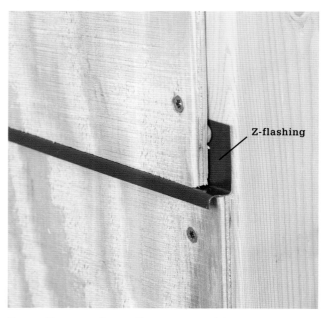

For walls over 8 feet tall, you can special order 9-ft. or 10-ft. panels, or use Z-flashing to join upper and lower panels. The flashing keeps water from getting in through the joint.

Install lap siding after the trim is up, overlapping each course by 1" or more. Nail cement board siding at the top. Wood siding is nailed just above the overlap.

CEDAR SHINGLE SIDING

Another relatively pricey but very attractive and lightweight option is cedar shingle siding. Tapered cedar shingles are typically sold in 16" and 24" lengths in random widths. They are installed over spaced, or "skip," sheathing: 1 × 2 or 1 × 3 boards fastened horizontally across the wall framing. Like lap siding, each course of cedar shingles overlaps the one below it. The amount of shingle left exposed is called the exposure. The spacing of the skip sheathing should be equal to the exposure.

Note: For a large or multi-story treehouse, you might need a base layer of plywood sheathing underneath cedar shingle siding, to give the wall sufficient shear strength; consult your local building department or a qualified building professional.

To install shingle siding, first add the skip sheathing or plywood, then the trim, then the siding. Install the skip sheathing over the wall framing with screws, spacing it according to the shingle exposure, which is determined by the length of your shingles: For 16" shingles, use a 6" to 7" exposure; for 24" shingles, an 8" to 11" exposure.

After the trim is up, begin the shingling with a double starter course along the bottom of the wall. Fasten the shingles with 5d siding nails or 1¼" narrow crown staples driven with a pneumatic staple gun. Overlap the vertical joints between shingles by at least 1¼". Install the remaining courses, overlapping each course below to create a uniform exposure. Fasten the shingles 1" to 2" above the exposure line of the succeeding course.

Butt together adjacent shingles, making sure that vertical joints are offset row-to-row and that amount of reveal is proportional to the shingle width.

Double starter course

Roof trim may include fascia—1× lumber that covers the sides of gable-end rafters and, if desired, the rafter ends along the eaves. A 1 × 2 along the top of the fascia adds definition and a nice transition line under the roof deck.

INSTALLING EXTERIOR TRIM

On a regular house, standard exterior trim is typically used to dress up wall corners, door and window openings, and roof edges. Adding simple trim elements is an easy way to create a finished look on a treehouse. On the other hand, if you want your house to look rustic or authentically kid-built, you may use little or no trim. The most common material for exterior trim is 1× cedar, available with either rough or smooth outside faces, but any rot-resistant or well-painted standard lumber will do. Install trim boards with galvanized box nails or siding nails.

Use 1 × 4 boards for outside wall corners, overlapping the boards with a butt joint. Inside (not interior) corners often get a single 2 × 2 board that fits against both adjacent walls.

Framed doors and windows can be trimmed with 1 × 2, 1 × 3, or 1 × 4 lumber to cover the joint between the jamb and the wall framing or siding. It usually looks best to leave a ¼" or so of the jamb exposed, creating a reveal.

Horizontal siding joints and similar seams can be covered with trim so they look like design elements instead of construction joints.

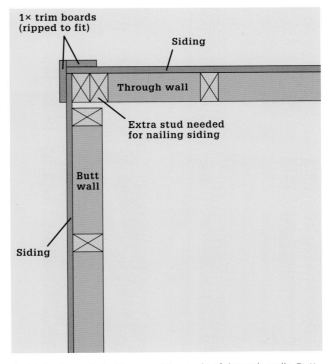

Cut trim boards to fit around the ends of through walls. Butt walls will appear to be trimmed when the walls are assembled.

Installing Walls

On an ordinary construction job, a wall raising is the day when a few extra helpers show up to tip up the walls and assemble the house frame. With a treehouse, wall raising gets a whole new meaning. It's time to call out your burliest neighbors, or get a little mechanical help from a block and tackle.

To get ready for the wall raising, snap chalk lines on the platform floor to represent the inside edges of the walls' bottom plates. With an accurate chalk line layout, you won't have to worry about squaring the walls as you assemble them.

For a small treehouse with light walls, lift two adjacent walls up onto the platform, set them on their chalk lines, and fasten them together through the end studs with 3" deck screws. Install the remaining walls one at a time, then anchor all of the walls to the platform floor framing with 3½" screws. Drive a few longer screws at floor joist locations.

For larger houses with heavy walls, lay one wall flat on the platform, then tip it up and set it on the chalk line. Anchor the wall's bottom plate to the platform with 3½" screws or 16d galvanized common nails, then add temporary 2 × 4 bracing to keep the wall upright. Hoist up the adjacent wall and fasten the bottom plate, then fasten the two walls together through the end studs. Repeat for the remaining two walls.

When all of the walls are up, cut out the bottom plate at the bottom of the door opening, using a handsaw.

Join the walls with screws driven through the end studs.

Top plates can be used to tie walls together at the corners, as well as provide a load-bearing surface for roof structures.

Building Railings

A railing is primarily a safety device. All too often, amateur and even professional designers (especially professional designers) see railings as an opportunity to get creative. The result is an unsuitable railing, which is essentially useless. Build a strong, solid railing with closely spaced balusters and you won't have to worry about who uses the treehouse, whether it's small children or tipsy adults. That means no ropes, no cables, and no twigs. Okay. Lecture over.

A good treehouse railing employs the basic construction details of a standard deck railing. Many treehouse railings are even simpler, eliminating features like the broad horizontal cap rail commonly found on house decks. The important thing is to adhere to the basic design requirements:

- Tops of railings must be at least 36" above the platform surface.
- Balusters (vertical spindles) may be spaced no more than 4" apart.
- Horizontal balusters are unsafe for children, who like to climb them.
- Railing posts (4 × 4 or larger lumber) may be spaced no more than 6 feet apart and must be anchored to the platform frame, not the decking.

- Top and bottom rails must be securely screwed to the posts, if possible on the inside faces of railing posts.
- Balusters should be fastened with screws; if nails are used, balusters must be on the inside of horizontal rails.
- All openings in railings—for access to the treehouse platform—must have a safety rail across the top.

To build a simple railing, cut 4 × 4 support posts to extend from the bottom edge (or close to the edge) of the platform's floor joists to 36" above the decking surface. Anchor the posts on the outside of the joists with pairs of ½" carriage bolts with washers. Install posts at the ends of railing runs, every 6 feet in between, and at both sides of access openings and stairways.

Cut 2 × 4 or 2 × 6 horizontal rails to span between the top ends of the posts. Fasten the rails to the inside faces of the posts with pairs of 3" deck screws. Continue the rail through access openings to create a safety barrier. Mark the baluster layout onto the outside faces of the rails, spacing the balusters no more than 4" apart. Cut 2 × 2 balusters to extend from the top of the rail down to the floor framing, overlapping the joists by at least 4". Fasten the balusters to the rails and joists with pairs of 2½" deck screws driven into pilot holes at each end.

The best railing is a simple one. Simple designs yield functional railings, providing a fair level of safety for those in the treehouse and peace of mind for those on the ground.

Finishing Interiors

In keeping with the rule that treehouses should be all about personal choice, the interior finishes present one of the best opportunities to create your own space—it's amazing how a little bit of paneling and trim can doll up the joint. At this stage, you want to ask yourself how the interior should feel: should it be tidy and refined like a house interior (or at least a summer cabin), or should it remain rustic and outdoorsy, something like a fire lookout tower?

Thinking about how you will use the treehouse will guide your choice of finishes as well as any functional features, like shelves and tables. On the other hand, you might decide to skip the interior finish altogether, string up a hammock, and get right down to business on an ideal treehouse pastime: napping.

Wall & Ceiling Paneling

Almost any wood paneling can work for interior treehouse walls and ceilings, including T&G boards, sheet paneling, plywood, and even knotty pine planks. Keep in mind that many paneling materials aren't intended for outdoor exposure, so if your interior isn't pretty well dried in (protected from rain), be prepared for some serious weathering. No big deal; after all, it is a treehouse.

TONGUE-AND-GROOVE PANELING

T&G paneling is a good choice for treehouses because it's pretty forgiving with temperature and moisture changes—it won't show gaps when the boards shrink with dry weather—and it strikes a nice balance with a finished yet rustic look. It's also easy to install over the typically less-than-perfect surfaces of a treehouse structure, allowing you to custom-cut small pieces to fit odd spaces, as opposed to having to trim large panels, as with sheet paneling.

You can install T&G paneling in a few different ways: running the boards horizontally or vertically over the entire wall or creating a wainscot effect by running them vertically over the first 32" or so from the floor, then running them horizontally up to the ceiling. The transition between the wainscot and upper paneling typically is covered with a band of trim or molding known as a chair rail. T&G paneling is equally appropriate for ceilings, and you can nail it directly over the rafters for a highly finished look.

Vertical T&G boards require blocking for nailing into. Install 2× lumber blocks between the studs every 2 or 3 ft. in each stud bay. For wainscoting, install blocking so that the top edge of the wainscot boards is centered on the blocks.

A 1 × 3 or 1 × 2 chair rail quickly hides the transition between a wainscot and the upper-wall paneling. If your door/window trim (page 112) is on top of the paneling, install the chair rail after the trim is up.

Blindnail T&G boards to the wall framing or roof rafters by nailing through the base of the tongue at an angle. The T&G joints hold the bottom edges of the boards in place and hide the nails along the tongue. Only the first and last boards in a run need nails through their faces.

SHEET PANELING

Sheet paneling installs quickly and is cheaper than board materials. The most popular type, beaded paneling, mimics the look of traditional T&G beadboard. It's commonly available in 4 × 8-foot sheets, sometimes in exterior grades for outdoor or high humidity areas—the best option for a treehouse.

If your sensibilities tend toward the modern, you can achieve a sleeker look with smooth marine plywood, a high-grade plywood made with waterproof glue. Sand the panels so they're smooth to the touch, and apply a clear finish of exterior polyurethane or furniture oil, if desired. Install the sheets with adhesive and nails (as with beadboard), use trimhead screws set just below the surface, or use exposed screws with finish washers.

Install beadboard paneling with construction adhesive and finish nails or paneling nails, running the panels vertically from floor to ceiling. The joints between panels should fall over the center of a stud.

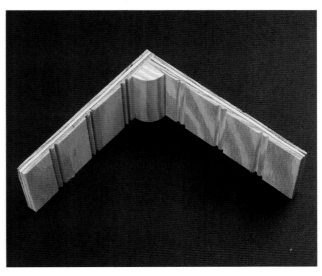

Trim along the edges where the panels meet the floor (or ceiling) with a 1 × 3 or any simple molding that matches the wood paneling. Use quarter-round to hide any gaps between panels at inside wall corners.

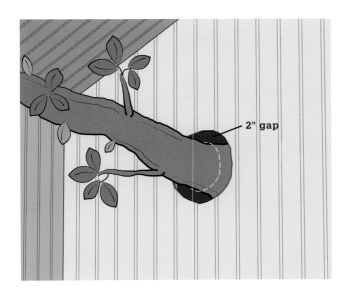

Mark paneling for custom cuts by scribing around the obstruction with a compass. Hold the panel or board in place and use the compass to mark the piece as it follows the contours of the obstruction. Remember to leave a 2" gap around any tree parts to allow for growth.

Ceilings look good with a finish of T&G boards or, for a rustic touch, rough-sawn cedar plywood. Run boards and panels perpendicular to the roof rafters. Install them using the same techniques used for wall paneling, starting at the walls and working up to the peak of the roof.

Shelves & Tables

Even the simplest enclosed treehouse can be made a touch more homey and certainly more functional with a few shelves and some kind of useable table surface. But with space at such a premium, standard bracketed shelves are probably overkill, and a secondhand coffee or bistro table might overwhelm the room. A custom built-in is a better way to go on both counts. You can size and configure any of the following designs to suit your needs.

2 × 4 SHELVES

These cheap and simple shelves are designed for unfinished interior walls, where they make good use of the empty spaces between wall studs. They can also make good use of scrap lumber left over from the treehouse build. 2 × 4 shelves are suitable for 2 × 2 and 2 × 3 wall framing. For 2 × 4 studs, use 2 × 6s for the shelves.

To make each shelf, cut a straight 2 × 4 to length so it spans across at least two neighboring wall studs, plus the desired amount of overhang on each end. For a custom look, you can angle the ends of the shelf back toward the rear edge with a 10° (or so) miter. Since the shelves protrude from the wall plane just a bit, it's a good idea to round-off the front corners with a ¾" or larger radius. Mark the radii with a compass or anything round, such as a small juice glass. Cut the rounded corners with a jigsaw.

Mark a level line across the front edges of the studs at each shelf location. To mark the notches for the studs, position each shelf board on its level lines so the board overhangs the outermost studs equally on both ends, then transfer both edges of each stud to the board. Measure the stud depth and transfer that to the board to mark the depth of each notch. Cut out the notches with a jigsaw.

To install the shelves, place each on its level lines and drill a single pilot hole through the shelf and each stud, with the hole centered on the edge of the shelf and the stud. Countersink the pilot holes for a finished look. Mount the shelves with 2½" deck screws.

Tools & Materials ▸

2 × 4 lumber	3" deck screws
2 × 6 lumber	Power drill & bits
Jigsaw	Eye and ear protection
Level	Work gloves
2½" deck screws	

2 × 4 shelves are easy to make and provide some much-needed wall space for favorite toys and games.

How to Build 2 × 4 Shelves

Draw level lines across the stud to represent the top face of each shelf. For wall studs spaced 24" on center, a good shelf length is about 33½", which yields a 4" overhang on the ends.

Mark the stud notches with the shelf board held in place. If a stud is twisted, hold a square or straightedge along the stud face to transfer the angle to the shelf board, or you can simply oversize the notch.

Fasten the shelves to the studs with screws. Use 2½" screws for 2 × 4 shelves with 2 × 3 studs. Use 3" screws for 2 × 4 shelves with 2 × 2 studs or 2 × 6 shelves with 2 × 4 studs.

CORNER SHELF

A rounded corner shelf makes a nice streamlined nook for a finished wall. And, as with the 2 × 4 shelves, you can probably make a few corner shelves with leftover material. Start with a piece of ¾" plywood (½" will work, too, if that's what you have), preferably with two adjacent factory edges making a 90° corner.

Draw the radiused front edge of the shelf, using a homemade compass (like the one shown on page 101 (Flip-up Table). A good size for this type of shelf is about 10" to 16", measuring from the rear corner to the front edge. Shelves larger than 16" or so might require a support bracket or a knee brace centered underneath the shelf. Cut the curved front edge of the shelf with a jigsaw, then smooth the curve and remove any rough or flat spots, as needed, with coarse sandpaper and a sanding block.

Use a level to mark the shelf location onto the two adjacent walls. These lines will represent the top edges of the 1 × 2 cleats, so the finished shelf surface will be ¾" above the lines. Cut two straight pieces of 1 × 2 to length about 2" shorter than the shelf depth to serve as the support cleats. If desired, round off or otherwise shape the front ends of the cleats for decorative effect. *Tip: If the cleats will go all the way into the wall corner (no corner trim), cut one of them ¾" shorter than the other. Install the longer cleat first, then butt the shorter one against the face of the longer. This way, both cleats will extend the same distance relative to the shelf.*

Fasten the cleats to the wall with deck screws or exterior drywall screws driven through countersunk pilot holes. The top edges of the cleats should be on the level lines. Set the shelf onto the cleats to test the fit against the walls. If the walls are out of square, scribe a cutting line along one side edge of the shelf, then trim the edge with a jigsaw or circular saw. Also notch the shelf corner to fit around any corner trim, as needed. Sand the shelf smooth and apply a finish, if desired. Install the shelf with 5d or 6d finish nails driven through the shelf and into the cleats.

A trusty light or other handy treehouse item will fit perfectly on the corner shelf.

How to Build a Corner Shelf

Install the cleats by screwing into the wall studs whenever possible. Otherwise, going into ⅝" or thicker board paneling or ⅜" or thicker plywood paneling should be plenty strong enough for a small shelf.

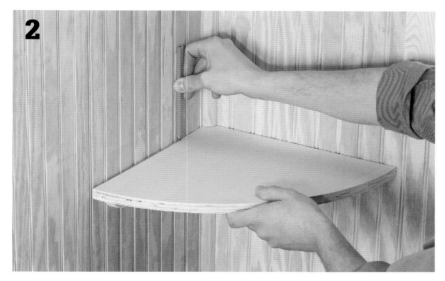

Eliminate unsightly gapping by scribing along one of the walls with a carpenter's pencil while holding the shelf tight to the adjacent wall. Trim along the scribed cut line, then check the fit.

Nail the shelf to the cleats with finish nails: Drill pilot holes (which have to be slightly angled, being so close to the wall), drive the nails, and set the nail heads just below the surface with a nail set.

FLIP-UP TABLE

Space-saving flip-up tables are popular features on boats, motor homes, and camping trailers, which means they're perfect for adding function in a treehouse. This table design includes a 48"-wide (24"-deep) semicircular table and a swing-out brace. Both pieces can be cut from a 4 × 4-foot half-sheet of ¾" plywood, and both are mounted with piano hinges. When swung down and out of the way, the table projects only about 1½" from the wall.

To cut the semicircular shape of the tabletop, mark the center along one edge of the plywood. Using an old wooden yardstick or a flat strip of wood, make a small notch in one end with a utility knife. Make a mark on the center of the stick, 24" from the bottom of the notch. Drill a small finish nail at the mark. Pin the stick to the plywood, just inside the marked edge, at the centerpoint. Using a pencil seated in the notch, rotate the stick to mark the semicircular cutting line. Cut out the tabletop with a jigsaw, and sand the edges smooth with coarse sandpaper and a sanding block.

Lay out and cut the swing-out brace from one of the remaining factory corners of the plywood sheet, following the diagram on page 101. Use the yardstick compass to draw the 10½" radius and a standard compass to draw the 2" radius at each end of the brace. Cut along the marked lines with a jigsaw, and sand the edges smooth. Apply a wood finish or paint the tabletop and brace, if desired.

Cut a straight 1 × 3 or 1 × 4 to length at 48½". This will become the ledger to which the tabletop hinge is mounted. Next, cut two lengths of piano hinge (a.k.a. continuous hinge), one at 48" and one at 20", using a hacksaw. Mount the piano hinge to the bottom face of the tabletop, using the provided screws. The plywood edge should come up to the hinge barrel but not overlap it. Fasten the other leaf of the hinge to the ledger so the leaf's edge is flush with the ledger's bottom edge. The ledger should extend slightly beyond the hinge at each end.

Mark a level line on the wall (or wall studs) to represent the top edge of the ledger, based on the desired tabletop height. With a helper, mount the ledger to the wall with 2½" deck screws driven into the wall studs. Install the 20" length of piano hinge to one side face of the swing-out brace, flush with the back edge of the brace. Mark the center of the ledger, along its bottom edge. Draw a plumb line down the wall at the mark. Mount the brace's other hinge leaf to the wall so the brace plywood is centered on the plumb line. The top edge of the brace should just clear the ledger above.

A flip-up table is just the thing when space is at a premium and important plans, puzzles, or popcorn needs a place to sit.

Test the tabletop and brace operation. Cut a 3"-long block from a scrap of 2 × 4 material. Use a circular saw and/or a chisel to cut a shallow channel down the center of the block, setting the depth so that the tabletop sits level when the block is placed between the tabletop and the swing-out brace. Fine-tune the fit, as needed, then fasten the block to the underside of the tabletop with 2" screws.

Make a Trammel ▸

Draw the rounded front edge of the tabletop with a homemade compass (also called a trammel). Using one of the plywood's factory edges as the straight rear edge of the top saves you from having to make this cut (which must be perfectly straight).

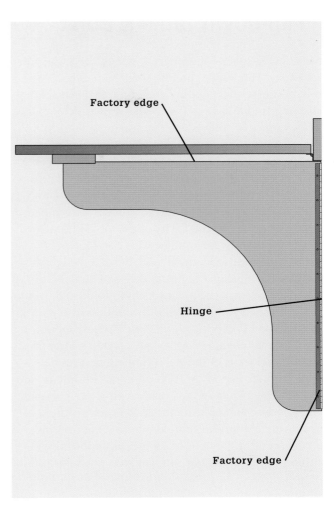

The swing-out brace has symmetrical curves cut into its front edge and uses the plywood's factory edges for its top and rear finished edges.

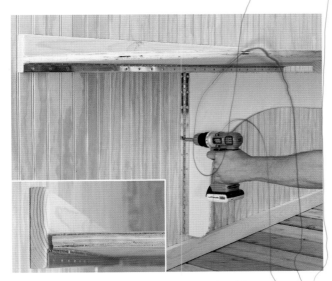

Mount the swing-out brace to the wall so it's centered under the tabletop. The barrel of the tabletop hinge should be on the inside of the hinge when installed (inset).

When the tabletop is up, the brace is captured inside the block's channel to keep the brace in position. Fine-tune the channel depth so the tabletop sits level before installing the block.

Flip-down Table & Bunk

Small living spaces often necessitate multifunctional furniture. This simple project singlehandedly covers the most essential needs of treehouse dwellers: eating, sleeping, and lounging. It's also a handy general work surface for things like conducting scientific experiments, writing memoirs, and mapping out plans for precision water balloon air strikes. In the upper position, the table unit sticks out only about 5½" from the wall. And the table surface quickly converts to a bed or lounge perch with the addition of a foam pad, which stores inside the cavity of the table's frame.

Construct the table frame with 2 × 4 lumber, making the width (depth) at least 24" and the length so it will accommodate the tallest sleeper. Cut two 2 × 4 side rails to match the finished length, and cut two ends to the finished width minus 3". Fit the side rails over the ends and fasten the pieces with 3" deck screws.

Cut the tabletop from ¾" plywood to match the outer dimensions of the 2 × 4 frame. For a smooth table surface, use AC or ACX plywood. Both have one smooth face, while ACX is made with water-resistant glue for outdoor applications. ACX is commonly sold as tongue-and-groove subflooring; you can use this if you cut off the tongue or groove, as applicable. If you're using a circular saw, cut from the C face (the ugly side) of the panel so any splintering occurs on what will be the bottom surface. Fasten the plywood top to the frame with 2" deck screws, using the panel's edges to square up the frame as you go.

Cut another 2 × 4 equal to the table length (or longer, as needed to meet wall studs); this is a ledger for mounting the hinges. Install three 3" (or larger) door hinges onto the top edge of the ledger and the top face of the tabletop. Use the provided screws if they seem suitable, or substitute with longer, heavy-shank wood screws for more strength. Pop out the hinge pins to separate the hinges, then mount the ledger to the wall studs with 3" deck screws, making sure it's level.

Tools & Materials ▸

2 × 4 lumber	Hinge and pins
3" deck screws	Bolts and nuts
¾" plywood	Chain
Circular saw	Foam padding
2" deck screws	Eye and ear protection
Power drill & bits	Work gloves

Enjoy an afternoon snooze on the flip-down bunk, then store the pad underneath and use the table to have fun all night.

How to Build a Flip-down Table & Bunk

Screw the plywood tabletop panel to the frame with the smooth face up. Drilling slightly countersunk pilot holes helps prevent deforming or splintering of the plywood for a smoother surface.

Install the ledger at the desired height for the tabletop. Standard table height is 29" to 30". If you go lower, make sure there's enough legroom under the table frame.

Support the tabletop with a strong steel chain bolted to the table frame and hooked onto screw hooks driven into the studs. Position the hooks so the table is level in the down position and both chains are equally taut.

Size the foam pad so it fits snugly into the frame cavity and won't fall out of its handy storage space.

Secure a length of chain to each end of the table, using a through bolt and nut. Attach the table to the ledger by assembling the hinges. Prop up the table so it sits level, then pull up each chain and install a heavy-duty screw hook into a stud or solid blocking so the chain is taut and forms about a 45° angle with the tabletop and wall.

Hold the table in the up position by hooking the chain links as close as possible to the tabletop. Measure the interior dimensions of the table frame and cut a piece of thick (up to 3½") foam padding to fit snugly into the frame cavity. Cover the padding with durable fabric, if desired.

Doors & Windows

Doors and windows for treehouses can range from holes cut in the wall to standard prehung units complete with weatherstripping and matching trim. Somewhere in the middle lie the most popular options: custom homemade units and salvage pieces, both of which are great for adding a little extra character and usually available at just the right price (preferably free). Doors and especially windows are a big part of what makes a treehouse fun for kids, so making homemade pieces is a perfect time to get the kids' creative input and have some fun with unconventional designs.

But before you get to the fun parts, here's a quick refresher course on door and window safety:

- Plastic glazing is much safer than glass and is recommended for all treehouse glazing. Polycarbonate is more resistant to UV damage than acrylic (Plexiglas) but more expensive.

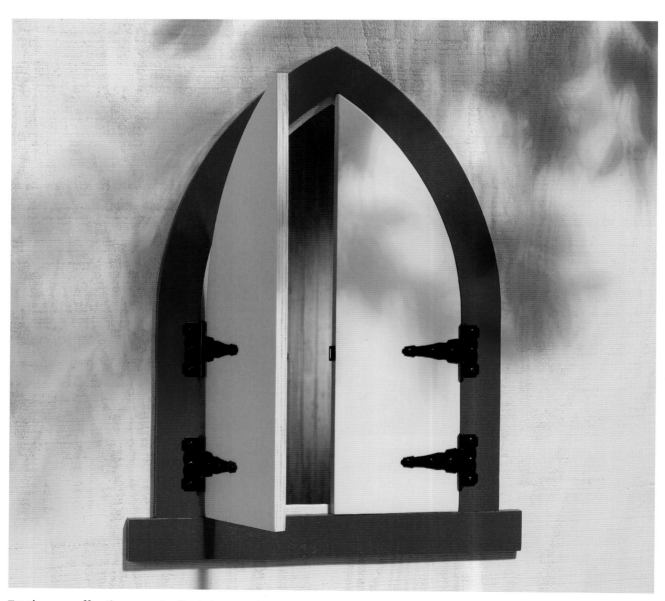

Treehouses offer the opportunity to let your imagination run wild, even in elements like doors and windows.

The natural light that windows provide can also embellish interior design choices, like these simple built-in shelves, country-style chairs, and log stool.

- Any glass used should be tempered or laminated. Stained glass or salvaged windows with very small panes might present an acceptable risk, and therefore an exception to this rule, but you can improve safety here with safety film or a protective panel of clear plastic glazing.
- Windows that open shouldn't be large enough to climb through unless they're located over a suitable deck or platform area. Kids are guaranteed to hang out of open windows (and let's face it, young people aren't very smart about physics and important things like gravity).
- Doors must have ample platform area on either side. It's usually safest for doors to open in to the treehouse, but some layouts dictate otherwise.

Now that the safety lesson is over, you can learn the basics of building a few different styles of homemade windows and doors that you can easily customize with a bit of creativity and the practical help of a good jigsaw.

Building a Window

It all starts with a simple square frame. Cut a 2 × 4 sill to equal the span of the window's rough opening, plus 2× the width of the exterior trim. The extra length is used to create "horns" that mate with the bottom ends of the trim on the outside of the wall. Cut a 15° slope into the top face of the sill, leaving a flat portion equal to the thickness of the wall framing. The angled cut should run the full length of the sill. (If you want to get fancy, create a drip edge underneath the sill with an ⅛"-deep saw cut.) Notch out the horns so the sill fits snugly inside the window opening, and fasten the sill to the rough opening sill with galvanized finish nails.

Option: You can use a 2 × 6 to create an extended ledge inside the window.

For the jambs, rip 1× lumber to match the wall thickness. If your framing is 2 × 2, you can use full-width pieces of 1 × 2 for the jambs. Cut the top jamb to span the top of the rough opening, and fasten it to the framing with finish nails. Cut and install the side jambs between the sill and top jamb.

Wrap the inside of the window frame with ½" quarter-round molding, to act as a stop for the glazing. Miter the molding at the corners, and nail it in place so its outside edge is flush with the outside of the

window frame. Cut ¼" polycarbonate glazing to fit the framed opening and set it against the stops with a bead of clear silicone caulk. Add an inner frame of quarter-round stops, sealed with caulk against the glazing and nailed to the jambs and sill.

If desired, add muntin bars (see page 107) made from ½" strips of wood. Join the bars at the window's center with a half-lap joint (made with opposing notches of equal size), and cope the ends to match the quarter-round window stops.

Sash Rehash ▸

To turn an old window sash into an operable window, build the same frame used for a fixed window, stopping after completing the sill and jambs. Mount the window sash to the side jamb with hinges so the window opens and closes freely. Then, add a frame of quarter-round stops snugged up against the inside of the window. Install a hook-and-eye latch or barrel bolt to secure the window when closed.

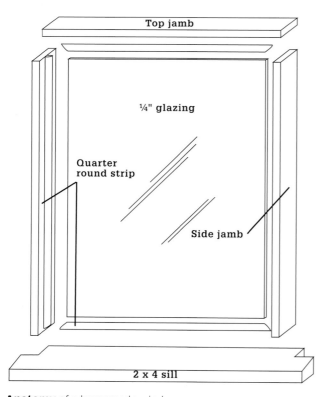

Anatomy of a homemade window.

Add trim to cover the edges of window and door jambs. Create a reveal by leaving a thin strip of jamb exposed.

Muntin bars add a nice traditional touch to glazed windows. Join the pieces with half-lap joints cut with a handsaw and chisel.

Salvaged windows and frames are perfect for treehouses, and are easily incorporated into existing design plans.

Homemade Window ▸

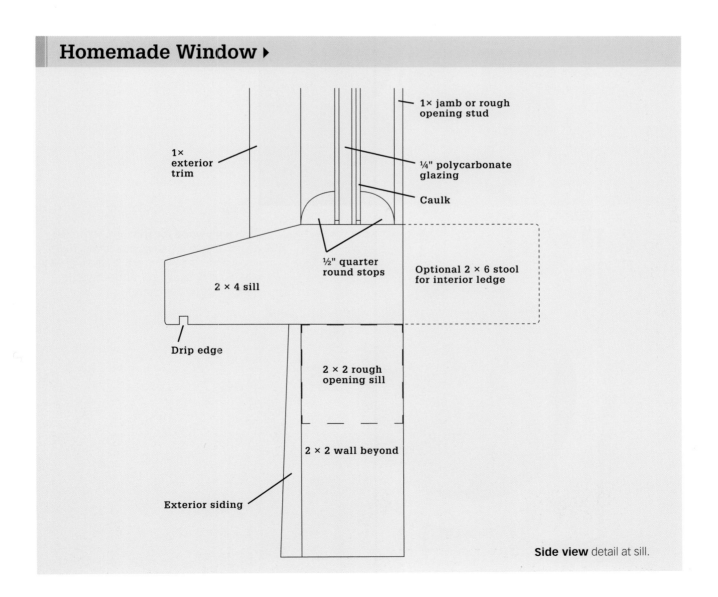

1× jamb or rough opening stud

1× exterior trim

¼" polycarbonate glazing

Caulk

½" quarter round stops

Optional 2 × 6 stool for interior ledge

2 × 4 sill

Drip edge

2 × 2 rough opening sill

2 × 2 wall beyond

Exterior siding

Side view detail at sill.

Window Cutouts

Another form of fixed window is a simple cutout made right into the exterior wall siding. You can glaze these with a plastic panel attached to the interior of the siding and add trim to either side, or you can leave them open to the breezes. Because there are no frames or hinges to worry about, you can make window cutouts highly decorative or intricate, depending on your jigsaw skills and the siding material. Plywood siding is the easiest to work with, and you can make the cutout in any area between framing members. Board siding usually needs framing around the edges of the opening to support the cut ends of the boards.

Cut out the siding in the window shape, using a jigsaw. *Tip: If framing gets in the way of the saw, transfer the outline to the exterior side (with the aid of small locator holes) where you can complete the cut.*

Use plywood for trim around circular and other oddly shaped windows. You can cut a round trim ring with a jigsaw or with a router and trammel, as described on page 141 (Button Swing).

To make a window cutout, draw the shape of the opening onto the interior face of the siding (so you won't accidentally overlap onto the framing). Add blocking as needed to support board siding. Drill a starter hole inside the marked cutout, then make the cut with a jigsaw. To prevent splintering along the cut edges, use an ultra-fine-tooth wood blade (around 20 teeth per inch) or "scroll" blade. These cut slower but much cleaner than standard blades.

Sand the cut edges to smooth out roughness and prevent splinters. If desired, cut a piece of acrylic or polycarbonate sheeting (see photo, below) to cover the opening and fasten it to the inside of the siding with short screws driven through oversized pilot holes (make the holes in the plastic a little bigger than the screws so the sheet can expand and contract without cracking). Seal the front of the plastic to the siding with a fine bead of clear exterior caulk. Add trim, if desired.

How to Make Window Cutouts

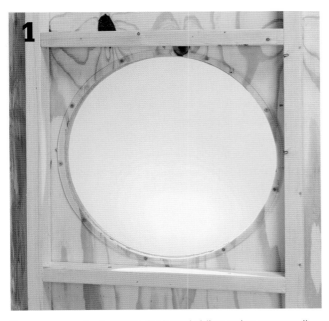

1

Frame around openings for board siding, using scrap wall-stud material. Blocking below the opening can serve as a small window sill.

2

Cutouts can be anything you want. If you're artistically challenged (like most of us), search online for a printable pattern that you can cut out and trace around to mark the outline onto the wall.

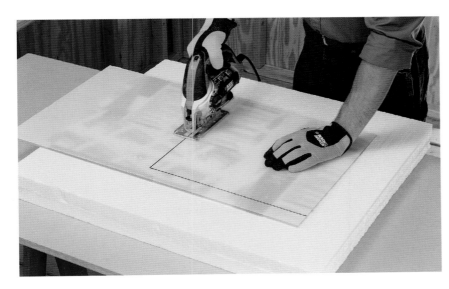

Tip: Cut plastic sheeting with a jigsaw and a 10 tpi (or finer) blade. To prevent cracking, lay the sheet onto rigid foam insulation board for support and cut through the foam and plastic at the same time.

Shutters & Pop-up Windows

These pop-up windows and shutters work like little doors and essentially follow the same design, apart from how they are hung. The windows are mounted horizontally on hinges and open upward, and the shutters are hung vertically and open out to the side. Both are good for opening up a treehouse to cool airflow and for battening down the hatches for campouts and rainstorms.

The best materials for these windows and shutters is exterior plywood and tongue-and-groove siding. You can also use standard board lumber (1 × 4, 1 × 6, etc.), but this can get a bit heavy and might show gaps between the boards. The size and shape are up to your imagination. Just make sure the hinges can be installed in a straight line and that they adequately support the weight of the window or shutter.

One interesting shape that works well for both single and double shutters is the Gothic arch. To make a set of double shutters (and matching trim) with plywood, start by laying out the doors onto a panel of ¾" or ⅝" exterior-grade plywood, using one of the panel's factory edges as the bottom edge of the doors. You will cut out both doors as a single piece, then cut down the center to create two matching doors. Be sure to leave a few inches of material at both sides of the door layout, from which you will cut the trim.

To lay out a Gothic arch, start with three parallel vertical lines: a long centerline and two flanking lines that represent the outside edges of the shutter doors. Draw a horizontal line between the two sides at the height where the arch will begin; this is line A-B, as shown the photo below. Set up a homemade compass (yardstick-style; see page 101) to match the length of line A. Place the pivot point of the compass at point A and draw an arch from B to C. Place the pivot point at B and draw an arch from A to C.

Lay out the arched trim before cutting out the door piece: Extend line A-B 2½" on each end, stopping at points D and E. Set the compass to the distance between A and E, and draw an arch between E and F, pivoting on point A. Move the pivot to point B, and draw arch D-F. Draw straight lines down from points D and E to complete the layout. The material removed during cutting will create the necessary gaps between the doors and the trim.

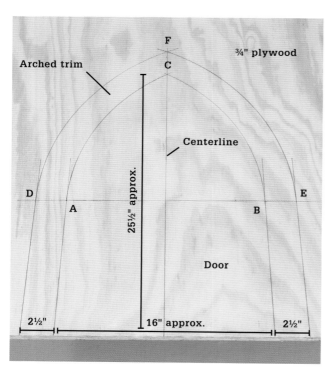

Draw the layout for the doors and arched trim, using a homemade compass to create the archs. The cut for the outsides of the doors also creates the inside profile of the arched trim.

Install the plywood trim with exterior screws or siding nails, exposing ½" of siding around the door opening on all sides.

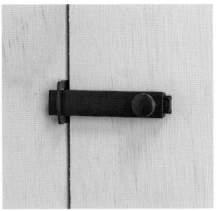

Mount the doors to the sides of the arched trim with the provided exterior-grade screws. Make sure the gapping between the doors and trim is even and consistent (left). A bolt or latch on the inside keeps the shutters closed (right).

Cut out the door piece with a jigsaw, cutting to the outside of your lines. Then, cut out the trim. Cut the doors down the centerline, using a circular saw or jigsaw and a straightedge guide to ensure a straight cut. Make this cut directly down the middle of the centerline to remove the same amount of material from both doors. Finally, cut a rectangular piece of base trim to the same width as the arched trim. The base can be flush with the outsides of the arched trim, or it can extend a little beyond, as desired.

Make the wall cutout for the shutters to match the shape of the doors as a single unit, but making it 1" narrower and shorter. This creates a ½" lip that the doors will close against. Install the arched trim on the outside face of the wall so the trim is centered over the wall cutout. Add the base trim. Hang the shutter doors with strap-style hinges (the kind with a hammered or antique look enhances the Gothic styling), mounting the hinges to the outside faces of the doors and arched trim. Add a flat hook-and-eye or slide-bar door latch to the inside faces of the doors so the shutters lock securely when closed.

Pop-up Windows ▶

Install pop-up windows just like shutters: Cut the opening 1" narrower and shorter than the window panel, add 1× board trim, and hang the window panel with hinges. A pivoting prop stick holds the window open, and a vertical barrel bolt latch secures it when closed.

Door & Window Trim. Doors and windows need trim to cover the joints or any gapping between the jambs of the door or window frame and the surrounding wall surface. For this reason, a little trim is a good idea even for simple, rustic structures. Without trim, doors and windows tend to look like a job that was never finished.

If you're paneling the interior walls of your treehouse, trim hides any gaps between the wall finish and the door and window frames. Gaps here are normal, because there's no sense in taking the time to fit the paneling perfectly to the jambs if you're covering the joints with trim.

Any 1× board lumber (1 × 2, 1 × 3, 1 × 4, etc.) is fine for treehouse trim. You can also rip down any T&G or other board paneling to make your own trim material. As a general rule, it looks best if all of the doors and windows have the same trim material and decorative detailing—a few of the classic joint options are shown here. Install trim with finish nails driven into the wall framing, and use a nail set to drive the nail heads slightly below the surface of the wood for a finished look.

Mitered trim corners are made with each piece cut at 45°, creating the classic picture frame effect. On windows with extended sills (stools; see photo below), only the top two corners are mitered. Hold the trim back from the jambs' edges to create a ⅛"-wide (or as desired) reveal.

Butted corners tend to look a little more rustic than mitered joints—and they're easier to make. You can cut the pieces so they're all flush on the outside or have the top piece overhang the sides, with or without a slight bevel on the ends.

A window sill traditionally has horns that extend beyond the jambs on both sides, creating a natural stopping point for the side pieces of the window trim, if your trim strategy includes side casing. The sill should slope away from the treehouse slightly to promote runoff of water.

Jamb

Horn

Fun Doors

Not to suggest that a Dutch door isn't fun…it's just that a door doesn't have to be rectangular. In fact, a door can be almost any shape as long as a good portion of the hinge side is straight and vertical—this is required for the hinges to work properly and ensure that the door is balanced (so it won't fly open or slam shut on its own).

Here's a fun arched door design that uses the exterior trim for a stop, which saves you from having to build an arched door frame. Both the door and the single, continuous trim piece are cut from a sheet of plywood. The little inset (Minnie-Me) door is a playful option that's built just like the full-size unit. If your taste leans toward Gothic arches more than round, follow the basic layout procedure for the Gothic arch shutters (page 110) to lay out the door and trim arches.

To build the rounded-arch door, lay out the door and trim pieces onto ¾" exterior-grade plywood. Draw three parallel lines marking the sides and centerline of the door (25" is a good minimum width for the door), then make a mark on the centerline to represent the top of the door. Set a homemade compass (yardstick-style; see page 101) to half of the door width. Using the same dimension, measure down from the top of the door and mark the centerline. Place the pivot nail of the compass on the new mark and draw the arch to complete the door shape.

On another part of the plywood sheet, lay out the trim, following the same process as with the door. Make the inner profile 1" narrower and ½" shorter than the door. Draw the outer profile 2½" outside the inner profile. Use the same techniques to mark the little inset door and trim at the desired size, centering the little door on the centerline of the main door. The arched trim for the little door is about ¾" wide and overlaps the opening about ¼" on the sides and top. The rectangular base trim is about 1" wide.

Cut out the main door with a jigsaw and a fine wood blade (to minimize splintering). To cut out the inset door, drill a small starter hole just below the bottom of the little door, then make the cutout, following your lines carefully. The cutout piece will become the door, and the starter hole will be covered by the base trim. Use the doors to check your layout of both arched trim pieces, then cut the trim with the jigsaw.

Cut the door opening into the wall siding, making it ½" larger than the door profile (see tip, page 114).

Install the main door trim with trimhead screws so the trim overlaps the door opening by ½" at both sides and along the arch. Using glue and brads, install the trim for the little door so it overlaps the opening at the sides and top but not the bottom. Install the base trim flush with the little door opening. Hang the little door to the main door with two small hinges mounted to the backsides of both doors. Add a small knob and a magnetic catch or a hook-and-eye latch to keep the little door closed.

Hang the main door with butt hinges screwed into the interior side of the door and siding. Use long screws on the siding-side of the hinges to penetrate the door trim for extra holding strength. Be sure to center the door in its opening so it clears the siding about ½" on both sides and about ¼" at the top and bottom. Add a door handle or gate latch to the door, as desired. It's best not to have a locking handle or latch on this door, lest you find yourself locked out of the treehouse in an emergency or when you need to retrieve a recalcitrant child.

Fun doors tend to be small, for kids, but it's a good idea to make them wide enough (at least 24") for adults to fit through.

Lay out the cut for the inset door (if you're making one), using a standard compass. Position the little door at the right height for kids to look through.

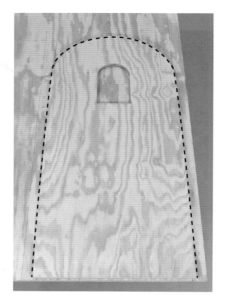

Test your trim layout using the cut door piece. When in doubt, you can trace around the door, then mark ½" inside the traced line to create the inner edge of the trim.

Cut out the door opening with a jigsaw. This matches the shape of the door but is offset by ½" to allow for a ½" clearance gap on both sides and ¼" at the top and bottom of the door.

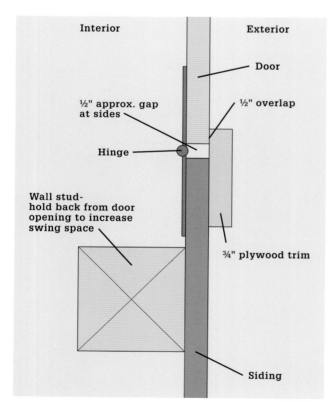

Interior   Exterior

Door

½" approx. gap at sides

½" overlap

Hinge

Wall stud- hold back from door opening to increase swing space

¾" plywood trim

Siding

Tip: If possible, leave some space between the hinge-side edge of the door cutout and the nearest wall stud. Because the door is mounted to the siding (instead of a door frame) an offset here allows the door to swing wider.

A door can add a lot of personality to a treehouse, so don't be afraid to get creative. You can do just about anything with a sheet of plywood and a jigsaw. All of the doors shown here work fine because the hinges are mounted along the straight sides.

Classic Doors

Here's how to build traditional Z-brace doors using board siding and standard 1× lumber. As with a window, start with a basic frame. Rip 1× lumber to equal the thickness of the wall frame, plus ¾". Cut the top jamb to span the top of the rough opening. Fasten the jamb to the header with galvanized finish nails so its outside edge is flush with the outside of the rough opening. Cut and install the side jambs to fit snugly between the top jamb and the floor.

Build the door to fit the dimensions of the new frame, leaving a ⅛" or so gap around the perimeter of the door. Be sure to factor in any offset created by the hinges when determining the door dimensions. Pine 1 × 6 T&G boards make great door material. Cut the boards to length and fit them together. Rip one or both side boards as needed to get the desired door width. Cut 1 × 6 Z-bracing to span across the door at the top and bottom hinge locations, then cut an angled piece to fit in between. For strength, the angled piece should point down to the bottom hinge. Assemble the door with screws driven through the Z-bracing and into the T&G boards.

To install the door, first add 1× trim along the inside of the door's rough opening, flush with the room-side edges of the jambs. Mount the door to the jambs using outdoor-type hinges, making sure the door opens and closes freely. *Note: As shown here, the door opens in to the treehouse interior. With the door closed, install ½" stops (cut from trim material) along the sides and top of the door. Add a gate latch or other handle to keep the door closed.*

You can use the same construction techniques to create a Dutch door. Build two short doors with a slight gap in between, and add a 1 × 4 shelf to the top of the lower door. Hang the door with two separate sets of hinges. Install a barrel bolt latch vertically onto the top door so the bolt extends down into a hole or plate in the bottom door's shelf.

A plain batten door made from 1 × 6 pine has a certain rustic charm. A single Z-brace stiffens the door, but adding a middle rail and second Z-brace prevents warping.

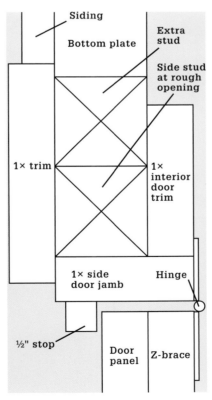

Siding

Bottom plate

Extra stud

Side stud at rough opening

1× trim

1× interior door trim

1× side door jamb

Hinge

½" stop

Door panel

Z-brace

Because DIY doors are not prehung, you'll need to build your own jambs and door stop using the basic configuration above.

A Dutch door has a top and a bottom that open independently (or together if you connect them).

Building Roofs

This is it. The home stretch. You're about to become a certified treehouse builder. Or certifiable, depending on how the project has gone. By now your hands are a little callused and your skills honed. That's good, because roof framing usually requires some experimentation and trial-and-error. Oh, yes, and patience.

If you framed your walls with extreme care and everything came out square and perfectly level, you could design your roof frame on paper and use mathematical calculations to find all the angles and locate the necessary cuts. But because you're building in a tree, it can safely be assumed that you improvised here and there and had to wing it on occasion, or you might not be the type who cares much for calculations. At any rate, most treehouse roof building works best with a cut-to-fit approach.

After the framing is done, you'll sheath the roof and install the roofing material. If the roof is free of intervening tree parts, you stand a good chance of keeping the interior of the house dry. If there are penetrations, you can try to seal them, but you should still find another place to store your signed copy of *Swiss Family Robinson*.

The structural members that support a treehouse roof generally don't need to be as beefy as the boards used for structures made with traditional building techniques. Here, a 1 × 6 ridge board provides adequate support while keeping down the weight of the treehouse.

Framing the Roof

The main structural members of any framed roof are the rafters—the lumber ribs that support the sheathing, or roof deck. On a gable roof, the rafters sit on top of the side walls and meet at a ridge board, or ridge beam, at the roof's peak. Rafters on hip roofs also form a peak, meeting at a ridge beam, or, more commonly in treehouses, at the tree's trunk. A shed roof has no peak, and the rafters simply span from wall to wall.

A roof's overall strength is determined primarily by the size of rafters and how closely they're spaced. Because treehouses tend to be small buildings, their roofs are typically built with 2 × 3 or 2 × 4 rafters spaced 16" or 24" on center. A small kids' treehouse might be fine with 2 × 2 rafters, while an arboreal palace, with rafter spans over 7 feet, might call for 2 × 6 framing. Snowfall is also a primary consideration in figuring rafter size. If you live in a snowy climate, check with the local building department for rafter span recommendations for your area.

CUTTING RAFTERS

The tricky part to framing any type of roof is figuring out the cuts where the rafters meet the walls and the peak. The cut at the peak is easy in theory: Its angle is equal to the pitch of the roof. If your end wall is built for a 30° roof pitch, the top ends of the rafters for this wall should be cut at 30°. In reality, this cut may need some adjusting, but the theoretical angle is the best starting point.

At the wall-end of the rafter a special cut called a bird's mouth allows the rafter to make level contact with the wall's top plate. The bird's mouth is made with two perpendicular saw cuts. The vertical cut, or heel, cut forms an angle with the bottom edge of the rafter that's equal to 90° minus the roof pitch (in our example: 90° − 30° = 60°). The horizontal, or seat, cut is level when the rafter is installed, and meets the bottom edge of the rafter at the same angle as the roof pitch. You don't have to memorize this geometry, but it helps to know the goal when cutting the bird's mouth to fit.

For each type of roof, make some conservative test cuts on a single "pattern" rafter, then adjust the cuts as needed through trial and error. When the rafter fits well on your house structure, use the pattern rafter as a template to mark the remaining rafters. If the rafters are tying into an uneven surface such as a tree part, cut and test-fit the remaining rafters one at a time.

To make a bird's mouth cut, mark the seat and heel cuts, using a rafter square to set the angles (see sidebar on page 120). Cut from one side with a circular saw, then flip the rafter over to complete the cuts, or use a handsaw. Don't overcut the lines to complete the cut, as this can significantly weaken small rafters.

The angles of a bird's mouth cut for a 30° roof pitch.

Cut the bird's mouth with a circular saw, cutting from both sides (or finishing with a handsaw) to avoid overcutting lines.

FRAMING A SHED ROOF

Congratulations. You've chosen the simplest and easiest roof of the lot. You'll be even happier with your choice when it's time to install the roofing. To frame your shed roof, mark the rafter layout onto the wall plates, working from one end wall to the other. For the layout, count the end-wall top plates as rafters; for these, you'll cut special rafters after the others are installed.

Cut a pattern rafter to length so it overhangs the side walls as desired to create a nicely proportioned eave. Set the rafter on the layout marks on top of the two side walls. Mark where both sides of each wall intersect with the rafter (on one side the rafter won't touch the plate, so you'll have to plane up from the wall with a straightedge). These marks represent the outside ends of the bird's mouth seat cut.

Use a rafter square to mark the bird's mouth cuts. Make the cuts and test-fit the rafter. Adjust the cuts as needed until the joints fit well on both walls, then use the pattern rafter to mark the remaining rafters.

Cut the rafters and fasten them to the wall plates with 16d galvanized common nails. At each joint, toenail two nails on one side of the rafter and one nail on the opposite side.

The two special outer rafters go right on top of the end-wall plates. Because they have no bird's mouth cuts, they must be ripped down so they're flush at the top with the other rafters. Use a level or straightedge to plane over from the adjacent rafters and measure down to the top plate to find the required depth for the outer rafters. Rip the outer rafters to size and fasten them to the top plates with 16d nails.

FRAMING A GABLE ROOF

The first step to framing a gable roof is preparing the ridge beam. The ridge beam gives you something to nail the rafter ends into and ties them all together for added stability. A 1 × 6 board makes a good ridge beam for 2 × 3 or 2 × 4 rafters. Cut the ridge beam to length so it spans the house between the inside faces of the gable-end walls.

Test-fit the pattern rafters on the walls, using a scrap piece to act as the ridge beam.

Toenail the rafters to the wall-top plates with three nails driven into the plates.

Level over from the inner rafters and measure to find the thickness of the outer rafters.

Install the outer rafters over the end-wall plates so the rafter ends meet at the roof peak.

Mark the rafter layout onto the ridge beam, working from one end to the other. For the layout, count the end-wall top plates as rafters; for these, you'll cut special rafters after the others are installed. Mark the layout onto both side faces of the beam. Hold the ridge beam next to each wall plate and transfer the layout onto the plate.

From this point, you'll need at least one helper until several of the rafters are installed. Cut two pattern rafters to length so they will overhang the side walls as desired to create a well proportioned eave. Using a scrap cut from the ridge beam, set the rafters on the side walls with the scrap held between their top ends. Mark where both sides of each wall intersect with the rafters (on the inside of the wall the rafter won't touch the plate, so you'll have to plane up from the wall with a straightedge). These marks represent the outside ends of the bird's mouth seat cut.

Use a rafter square to mark the bird's mouth cuts. Make the cuts and test-fit the rafters. Adjust the cuts as needed until the joints fit well on both walls, then use the pattern rafters to mark the remaining rafters. Starting at one end of the house, install two opposing rafters with the ridge beam in between so the top ends of the rafters are flush with the top edge of the beam (you can temporarily tack the other end of the ridge to the far wall to hold it up while you work). Toenail the rafters to the wall plates with two 16d galvanized common nails on one side of the rafter and one nail on the other side. At the top ends, toenail through the rafters and ridge with three 10d nails. Repeat to install the remaining pairs of rafters.

The four special outer rafters install on top of the end-wall plates. They have no bird's mouth cuts, so they must be ripped down so their tops sit flush with the tops of the other rafters. Use a level or straightedge to plane over from the adjacent rafters and measure down to the end-wall top plates to find the required depth of the outer rafters. The outer rafters will meet together at the peak, without the ridge beam in between. Rip the outer rafters to size and fasten them to the top plates with 16d nails.

FRAMING A HIP ROOF

A simple hip roof has the perfect shape for capping off a square treehouse surrounding a central trunk. Since the roof pitch has yet to be determined, first pick an angle that looks good to you—let's say 40°. Cut one end of a pattern rafter at 40°. Use a handsaw or circular saw to bevel the edge of one of the outside wall corners at 40°. This creates a flat surface for receiving the rafter. Set the rafter on the wall and the tree. If everything looks good, mark where the top of the rafter meets the tree. Use a level to extend this mark around the perimeter of the trunk.

Using the pattern rafter, mark the cuts for three more corner rafters (the hip rafters). Cut off the remaining three wall corners to match the first. Install the four hip rafters so their top ends are on the tree marking and their bottom ends rest on the walls. Fasten the rafters to the tree with 3½" galvanized wood screws; fasten to the walls with screws or 16d galvanized common nails. Drive two toenails (or screws) on one side of the rafter and one nail on the other side.

To cut the interior, or common, rafters, set up two mason's lines: one line running between the tops of the hip rafters, directly above where they meet the walls, and one line strung around the ends of the hip rafter tails. Use the lines for reference as you cut the common rafters to fit the structure. Mark the common rafter layout onto the top wall plates, centering a full-length rafter between each pair of hip rafters. You'll probably also need two or more short rafters that run from the hip rafters to the walls. These are called jack rafters.

The commons and jacks get a bird's mouth cut to rest on top of the wall. Cut and test-fit the rafters one at a time, using the strings to help with measurements. Cut the common rafters long to start with, then miter the top ends to fit roughly to the tree, followed by the bird's mouth. To cut the jack rafters, bevel the top ends to fit flush against the side faces of the hip rafters. This can be a difficult cut, but it doesn't have to be perfect; just get it close enough to make a strong joint. When all joints fit well, cut the bottom end of each rafter to length so it meets the outer mason's line. Fasten the rafters as you fastened the hip rafters.

A Square for the Hip ▸

A rafter square (also called a speed square) is a handy tool for marking angled cuts using the degree of the cut or the roof slope. Set the square flange against the board edge and align the pivot point with the top of the cut. Pivot the square until the board edge is aligned with the desired degree marking or the rise of the roof slope, indicated in the row of common numbers. Mark along the right-angle edge of the square.

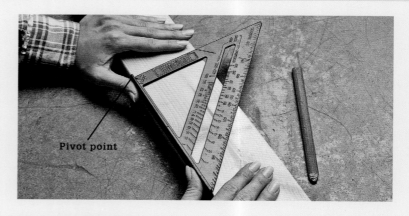

Pivot point

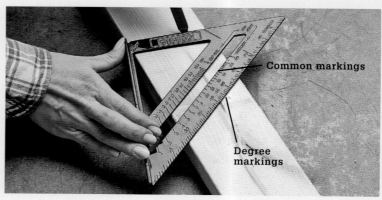

Common markings

Degree markings

A clipped corner has part of the siding and cap plate cut away so the hip rafter can sit squarely on top of the wall.

String mason's lines from rafter tip to rafter tip and test with a line level to make sure that the rafters are all level with one another.

Hip rafter (typ.)

Jack rafter (typ.)

Fasten the top ends of the jack rafters to the sides of the hip rafters.

Sheathing & Roofing

If you've ever built a shed or even a doghouse, you know that roofing a small building can be particularly satisfying. You get to learn and practice basic roofing skills without the backbreaking work of endless roof expanses. The same is true for treehouses.

The first step is choosing a roofing material, and that will determine what you'll use for the roof deck, or sheathing. If you're building a small treehouse, you might want to take the easy route and use a couple of sheets of plywood as the sheathing and the roofing. On any house with a gable or shed roof, consider adding 1× trim up against the underside of the roof sheathing along the end walls, to hide the faces of the outer rafters.

ASPHALT SHINGLES

Asphalt shingles are cheap, durable, and easy to install. They're laid over plywood sheathing and a layer of 15-pound building paper. They are, however, the heaviest of the standard roofing materials and might not be the best choice if you're trying to minimize weight.

Plywood roof decking is the fastest and usually cheapest type of decking to install. Make sure the plywood you use is rated for use in roofing. If you'll be installing asphalt shingles, a plywood deck is the way to go.

To install an asphalt shingle roof, start with a single layer of ½" exterior-grade plywood sheathing. Working up from the ends of the rafters, fasten the sheathing to the rafters with 8d galvanized box nails, driven every 6" along the edges and every 12" in the field of the sheets. Overhang the rafter sides and ends as desired. Leave extra overhang at the sides of the outer rafters if you plan to install trim there. Cut the plywood as needed so vertical joints between sheets break on the center of a rafter, and stagger the vertical joints between rows.

Add the building paper, overhanging the sheathing along the eave by ⅜". For a hip roof, also overhang the hip ridges by at least 6". Secure the paper to the sheathing with staples. Install the remaining rows, overlapping the row below by at least 2", and overlap any vertical joints by at least 4". On a gable, overlap the roof peak by 6", then install paper on the other side, working up from the eave.

Begin the shingle installation with a starter course: Snap a chalk line 11½" up from the eave (for standard 12"-wide shingles). Cut off half (6") of the end tab on the first shingle and position the shingle upside down so the tabs are on the chalk line. Overhang the side edge (on gable and shed roofs) by ⅜". Fasten the shingle with four 2d roofing nails, about 3½" from the bottom edge. Install the rest of the starter row in the same manner, using full shingles and butting their ends together.

Note: For a hip roof, completely shingle one roof section at a time, trimming the shingles along the hip peaks before moving on to the next section.

Install the next course directly on top of the starter course but with the tabs pointing down. Begin with a full shingle to establish a 6" (half-tab) overlap of the tabs between courses. Use four nails for each shingle: one nail ⅝" above each tab and one nail 1" in from both ends. For each successive course, snap a chalk line 17" up from the bottom of the last installed course; this helps you keep the shingles straight and maintains an even 5" exposure. Overhang the first shingle in each course by a half tab until you get to a 1½-tab overhang, then start over with a full shingle.

To shingle the peaks of gable and hip roofs, cut ridge cap pieces from full shingles, as shown in the photo (page 123). Cut one cap for every 5" of ridge. Center the caps over the ridge and fasten them with two nails.

Start installing asphalt three-tab shingles from the eave area of the roof and work your way up toward the peak. If you've never shingled a roof before, make sure to get some experienced help or at least plenty of good information before attempting it.

When the field shingles are all in, cut three cap shingles from each three-tab shingle, tapering the side edges slightly as shown (inset). Nail the caps over the ridge so the nails are covered by the next cap.

Roof, Meet Tree ▸

When roofs leak on regular houses, it's almost always the result of introducing foreign objects—plumbing vents, skylights, dormers, meteorites, you name it. Well, a tree is a very foreign object to a roof, and a large penetrating branch or trunk makes sealing the roof an ongoing challenge. But it can be done. Your best bet is to wrap around the tree and over the top of the penetration with overlapping pieces of neoprene rubber (the stuff used in wetsuits). Seal the neoprene to the tree with a compatible roofing or gutter sealant. Keep some extra sealant handy for routine spot checks. Clear roof cement, such as the Through the Roof product at right (see Resources) can be used to fill small gaps invisibly. Because it is roof cement, it will remain flexible over time so it doesn't crack.

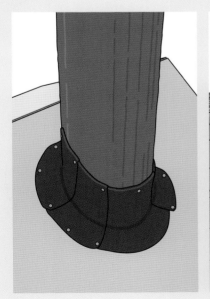 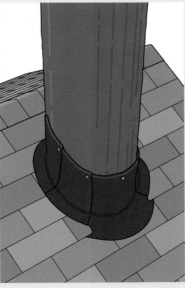

When the roof deck is installed, wrap pieces of 3/16"-thick neoprene around the penetrating tree part, overlapping onto the tree, the decking, and the other neoprene pieces. Test-fit the pieces as you work, without using sealant. When you're sure the leak is covered, Install the collar pieces one at a time, starting at the lowest point of the roof deck and working up and around the tree. Overlap the upper pieces onto the lower pieces, as with roof shingles. Seal all edges of the neoprene with a liberal application of roofing cement or gutter sealant. Tack the pieces to the tree with a few deck screws, as needed. Complete the roof installation as normal, overlapping the shingles onto the neoprene pieces at the sides and top of the tree, and seal around the shingles if necessary.

Cedar roof shingles look terrific up in a tree. Installing them is very similar to installing shingles for siding. Be sure to read the shingle manufacturer's directions carefully to find recommended exposures and installation practices.

The peak of a roof created with wood shingles will naturally have a seam that needs covering. The easiest way to do this is by beveling two pieces of ridge trim so one piece fits over the other piece.

CEDAR SHINGLES

Installing a cedar shingle roof is almost identical to siding a wall with cedar shingles, which is covered in detail on page 89. The few differences for a roof application are explained here. *Note: Don't use cedar shingles on roofs with less than a 3-in-12 pitch (about 14°).*

Sheath the roof with 1 × 4 skip sheathing, spacing the boards to equal the shingle exposure. Follow the shingle manufacturer's recommended exposure for the size and grade of your shingles and the roof slope.

Install a double starter course of shingles along the eave, overhanging the roof edge by 1-1½" at the eave and 1" at the side. Leave a ¼" gap between adjacent shingles to allow for expansion, and overlap the gaps by at least 1½" between courses.

To complete the peak of a gable roof, layer strips of 15-pound building paper (tar paper) into the last two courses of shingles, as shown in the photo (above). Cap the peak with custom-beveled 1× trim boards or pre-made ridge caps. Cap the ridges on a hip roof with pre-made ridge caps.

METAL OR PLASTIC ROOFING

With its history as a popular roof material for farm buildings and cabins, corrugated roofing has the right character for treehouses. The material usually comes in 2-foot wide panels in various lengths. Order panels long enough to span each roof section so you won't have to deal with horizontal joints. Installation of corrugated roofing is specific to the type and manufacturer of the panels you use, and you should follow the manufacturer's instructions carefully.

Here is a general overview to give you an idea of the roofing process: Start by installing 1× or 2× lumber purlins perpendicular to the rafters. Fasten the roofing panels to the purlins with screws or nails fitted with self-sealing rubber washers. Overlap adjacent panels at the ribs, then fasten through both panels to seal the seam. Cap roof ridges with a preformed ridge cap, sealing it to the roofing panels with a sealer strip and caulk.

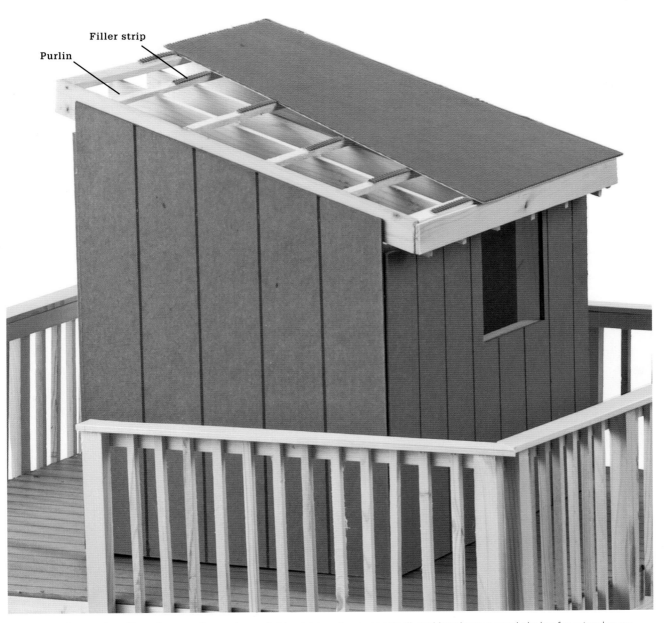

Filler strip

Purlin

Corrugated metal or fiberglass roof panels are lightweight and easy to install, making them a good choice for a treehouse. They are usually installed over foam or plastic filler strips that have the same profile as the roof panels. The filler strips are attached to boards (called purlins) that fit between the roof rafters.

Modes of Access

Getting from point A to point B can be half the fun of a treehouse. It's one of the things that separates treehouses from other hangouts and play areas. With a little creative thinking, you can devise all kinds of access points and build your own conveyances using standard materials. It's also fun to check out the equipment available through specialty dealers.

So, what's going to be your mode of access? Kids will usually choose the more adventurous routes, like climbing ropes or zip lines. Then again, kids ride bikes with their eyes closed. For you, perhaps a flat-rung ladder is a better choice for balancing ease-of-use and out-of-the-ordinary. Often a combination of travel options is best—maybe a ladder for getting up to the treehouse with an armload of stuff, and a fireman's pole for swashbuckling exits.

A traditional staircase is also an option, and a good idea for anyone with limited agility or for treehouses that receive lots of regular traffic.

Ladders

A handmade, permanently attached wood ladder is perhaps the best all-around means of access for a treehouse. Two good ladder designs are the double-rung and the flat-rung, both of which are suitable for primary means of access. The rope ladder, a kids' favorite, is more difficult to use and serves better as a fun, secondary route.

DOUBLE-RUNG LADDER

This ladder works much like an extension ladder but with greater foot stability offered by the doubled rungs. To build the ladder, start with two long, straight 2 × 6s that are relatively knot-free. These are used for the stringers (side uprights) of the ladder. Set one of the boards on the ground, and lean it against the treehouse platform at an angle that looks comfortable for climbing—60° to 70° is a good range for most situations; we'll use 65° for this example.

Cut the bottom ends of the stringers at 65°. Lean them against the platform at 65° and mark the top ends for cutting. When the ladder is finished, you can fasten the stringers to the platform or to railing posts at either side of the ladder landing. At this point, decide whether the stringers should stop flush with

The idea of a firepole may fill you with alarm, but kids love them. If you provide supervision and a soft landing place you'll find that a firepole may become the preferred method for exiting (or even entering) a treehouse.

A double-rung ladder employs pairs of 1½" dowels at each step to create a more stable stepping point. The dowels are glued (with a water-resistant adhesive such as polyurethane glue) into 1"-deep holes in the stringers.

Clamp and glue the doubled rungs as you go. If you space the rung pairs at roughly 12" intervals you should have sufficient flex in the stringers so you can successfully insert each new pair without unclamping the preceding pair.

the platform surface or extend above the platform to serve as handholds. Cut the top ends of the stringers, rounding them over or squaring off, as desired. The stringers must be identical in length and shape.

Mark the rung layout onto the front edge of one of the stringers, marking every 10" to 12" and starting at the bottom, front end of the stringer. Standard rung spacing is 12", but 10" is more comfortable for kids. Make sure the spacing is uniform over the entire layout. Place the stringers together and transfer the rung layout to the unmarked stringer. Extend each layout mark across the inside face of each stringer at 65°, using a rafter square or a template cut at 65°.

Measure 1¾" in from the front and rear edges of the stringers and mark the rung centers on each layout line. *Note: This measurement is for a 1½"-diameter dowel. Cut the rungs to length at 20". This gives you a useable rung width of 18" and a total*

ladder width of 21". At each rung centerpoint, drill a 1½"-diameter × 1"-deep hole, using a spade bit marked with masking tape to gauge the hole depth. Test-fit several rungs to make sure they fit snugly in the holes.

Lay out all the parts so everything's ready for the glue-up. Working on one stringer, coat the insides of the rung holes with waterproof wood glue; avoid filling up the holes with excess glue, as this will prevent the dowels from setting to full depth. Seat the dowels completely in the holes, using a rubber mallet, if necessary. Make sure each dowel is perpendicular to the stringer. When all dowels are in, glue up the other stringer (it helps to have another person working ahead of you) and set it over the dowel ends, completely seating them in the holes. Clamp the stringers so the ladder is square, and let the glue dry. Secure the completed ladder to the treehouse platform or railing posts with screws.

FLAT-RUNG LADDER

A flat-rung ladder feels a little more like a staircase and is a little easier to climb than a standard ladder. However, for safety, climbers should always face the ladder when going up or down. An optional handrail on each side is a good idea for additional safety. To build a flat-rung ladder, follow the steps given for the double-rung ladder (page 126) to establish the ladder angle, cut the 2 × 6 stringers, and mark the rung layout. For the flat-rung ladder, the layout lines for the rungs represent the top of each rung.

Cut 2 × 4 or 2 × 6 rungs to length at 18". This gives you a total ladder width of 21". Fasten each rung with three 3½" galvanized deck screws driven through pilot holes in the outside of each stringer and into the ends of the rungs. Make sure the top of the rung is on the layout line and its back edge is just touching the back edges of the stringers. Reinforce each rung connection with a 1 × 2 cleat. The cleats should extend from just behind the rung's front edge to the rear edge of the stringers. Fasten the cleats with 2" screws driven through pilot holes in the cleats and into the stringers.

To add handrails, cut 3"-long blocks from 2 × 2 lumber, and sand all edges smooth. Install the blocks on the front edges of the stringers at 36" intervals, using pairs of 3½" screws. For the railing, install 1¼" or 1½"-diameter dowel rods centered side-to-side on the blocks. Fasten through the railing and into the blocks with 3½" screws driven through counterbored pilot holes. Make sure all screw heads are below the surface of the railing. If you need more than one wood dowel rod for each side of the railing, butt the railing pieces together over the center of a block, and pin the ends together with a couple of angled finish nails to ensure a smooth transition.

Fasten the rungs to the stringers, then back up each rung with a pair of 1 × 2 cleats.

Countersink the railing screws so there's nothing protruding above the railing surface.

Not your everyday ladder. Rope ladders take a little getting used to, but they're a lot of fun. They're easiest and safest to use when they're anchored at the bottom to prevent swaying (you can snap the ladder onto the anchor with a carabiner so it can be pulled up into the treehouse if desired).

ROPE LADDERS

Rope ladders can be a little tricky to climb, but that's what makes them fun. Kids can pretend that they're scaling up the rigging of a pirate's ship to reach the crow's nest atop the main mast. A handy trick for making a rope ladder more stable is to secure the bottom end to the ground. Once you've hung the ladder, tie the two rope ends together at the bottom with a locking carabiner attached. Clip the carabiner into an eye bolt set in some concrete in the ground. You can easily unclip the carabiner to pull up the ladder into the treehouse.

To make a rope ladder, cut two lengths of ¾" nylon or manila rope, including several extra feet of slack.

For the rungs, cut 1 × 4 boards or 1½"-diameter wood dowels at 21". You'll need one rung for every 10" of vertical rise of the ladder. Drill a ¾" hole through each rung, 2" in from each end and centered side-to-side on the rung. Leaving plenty of slack for tying off the rope ends, mark the ropes every 10". Working from the top down, thread each rung onto the ropes and tie a simple knot below the rung so the top of the rung is on the layout lines. Repeat to install the remaining rungs.

Secure the top ends of the ladder ropes to the treehouse's platform framing, railing, or overhead beams using a bowline knot on each rope. If desired, anchor the bottom end of the ladder to the ground, as described above.

Stairs

Basic carpentry and math skills are all you need to build a fine staircase to the treehouse. See page 131 for a schematic cutaway of this design.

Traditional stairs might be a preferable mode of treehouse access for any number of reasons. They're safer and easier to climb than a ladder or ladder steps. They're also a good idea for treehouses that are used for work or other activities that frequently require hauling supplies (or lunch) up and down.

While stairs inside your house and those serving attached decks and the like are strictly governed by building codes, the design specifications for treehouse stairs typically aren't as stringent. You might choose to build your steps narrower than the standard 36" minimum or to make them a bit steeper to save space. However, be sure to include strong railings all the way up and to make the steps uniform in height and depth. An unexpected variation in step size will always trip you up, if not worse.

The stairbuilding technique outlined here is a simplified version of how most carpenters do it.

The basic construction involves two relatively short flights of stairs joined by a small landing. You can use the same methods described to build a longer set of single-flight stairs, but landings are recommended for any staircase with more than 12 steps total. For staircases that rise well over 8 feet and require more than one landing, consult a building pro for help with the staircase design and construction.

A staircase can be particularly useful for the treehouse build, and you can construct the stairs as soon as the treehouse platform is complete. However, if there's any chance that your kids and neighborhood youngsters will find their way up the stairs before the house is finished, don't build the stairs until the platform railing is complete and there isn't any place around the platform where an unwitting (or witless) person could get hurt or fall. Also be sure to rope off or barricade a staircase when you're not around during the construction phase.

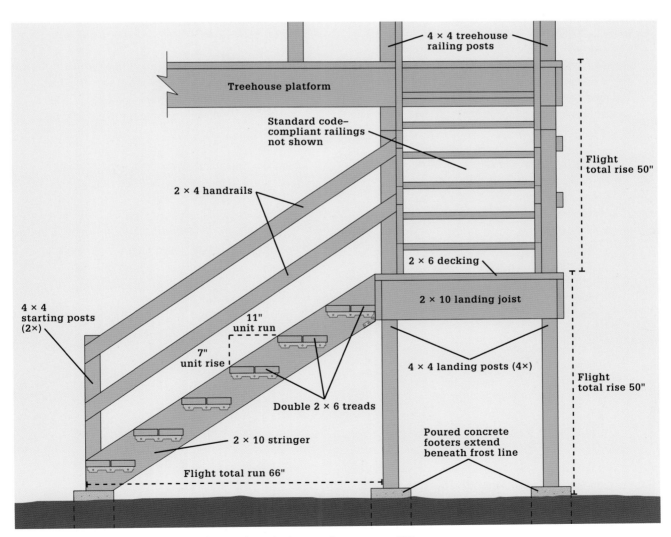

4 × 4 treehouse railing posts

Treehouse platform

Standard code-compliant railings not shown

Flight total rise 50"

2 × 4 handrails

2 × 6 decking

2 × 10 landing joist

4 × 4 starting posts (2×)

11" unit run

7" unit rise

Double 2 × 6 treads

4 × 4 landing posts (4×)

2 × 10 stringer

Flight total rise 50"

Poured concrete footers extend beneath frost line

Flight total run 66"

Cutaway view of stair path. To see how stair teminology works, see page 132.

Understanding Stair Terminology ▸

Stairs are laid out using the following dimensions, most of which are measured on-site and adjusted to fit the installation:

Total rise: the vertical distance between the lower level (bottom of stairs; in this case, the ground) to the upper level (top of stairs; the treehouse platform).

Total run: the horizontal distance between the bottom and the top of the stairs.

Unit rise: the vertical distance from the top of one step tread to the top of the next tread.

Unit run: the horizontal distance from the front edge of one tread to the front edge of the next tread.

On stairs with landings (more than one flight), the total rise is the combined rise dimensions of the flights; the total run is the combined run dimensions, not counting the landing.

CALCULATING STAIR PARTS

Figuring the dimensions for laying out basic stairs is a straightforward process using simple math, but it does involve several steps. Stair calculations also can vary, based on the staircase design, the site, and the desired size of the steps. The following is a simplified method for figuring dimensions for the stairs shown here, using a standard tread depth (unit run) of 11" and an approximate step height (unit rise) of 7".

1. Find the approximate total rise of the staircase by measuring from the ground to the top of the treehouse platform. You will take a more accurate measurement that accounts for ground elevation later in the process.

   As an example, the platform on page 131 is 96" above the ground. Therefore:

   Approximate total rise = 96"

2. Find the approximate total run of the stairs by multiplying the total rise by the rise-run ratio. For 7"-tall, 11"-deep steps, the rise-run ratio is 1.57 (11 ÷ 7 = 1.57).

   Ex: 96" (approx. total rise) × 1.57 = 151" (rounded up)

   Because a staircase (or flight) always has one fewer run units than rise units, subtract two rise units (one for each flight) from the total run.

   Ex: 151 − 22 = 129"

3. Find the actual total rise: First, divide the approx. total run by 2.

   Ex: 129 ÷ 2 = 65" (rounded up)

   Use this dimension to roughly lay out the stair path. Starting at a point even with the treehouse platform, measure out a right angle on the ground, with each leg of the angle at 65", as shown on page 131. Then, use a long, straight board to level over from the treehouse platform to the bottom-of-staircase location. Measure between the board and the ground at this spot to find the actual total rise of the staircase.

   Find the approximate location of the bottom end of the staircase by plotting the stair path (see illustration). Level over from the platform (top of stairs) to a point directly above the bottom of the stairs, then measure for the total rise.

4. Use the accurate total rise to calculate the final stair elements. For our example, the ground slopes down a bit from the treehouse, so the actual total rise is 100". Therefore:

   Number of steps (including landing and treehouse platform): total rise ÷ 7 (standard rise unit)

   100 ÷ 7 = 14.29. Round down to 14.

   Unit rise (height of each step): total rise ÷ number of steps

   100 ÷ 14 = 7.14, or 7⅛".

   Total run: total rise × rise-run ratio − two rise units

   rise-run ratio: 11 ÷ 7.14 = 1.54

   100 × 1.54 = 154

   154 − 22 = 132

   Total run per flight: 66" (132 ÷ 2)

   Total rise per flight: 50" (100 ÷ 2)

CONSTRUCTION NOTES

Once you've calculated the stair dimensions, you can lay out and install the landing posts. Locate the house-side edge of the landing at half the distance of the total run—66" in our example. The posts will go inside the landing's joist frame, so install them 1½" inside the footprint of the landing on all four sides.

For each post, dig a 12"-diameter hole at least 42" deep (or as needed to extend 6" below the frost line). Add 6" of compactible gravel to the bottom of the hole and tamp it down. Locate the two starting posts with the bottom end of the first-flight run and aligned with the landing posts. The starting posts should extend at least 43" above the ground.

Mark the top of the finished landing onto the four landing posts. This should be exactly half of the total rise for the entire staircase. Cut four 2 × 10 joists to wrap around the outsides of the posts. Install these 1½" below the marks, fastening to the posts with pairs of lag screws with washers. Cover the joists with 2 × 6 decking, spacing the boards about ¼" apart for drainage. Make sure the decking is flush with the outsides of the joist frame on the two sides that will receive the stair stringers.

INSTALLING THE STAIR ANGLES & STRINGERS

Install the metal stair angles onto the inside faces of both stringers, centering the angles under each tread marking. *Note: One commonly available type of stair angle has three screw holes on one flange and four on the other. You can invert the angle so the four-hole flange is against the tread boards, allowing you to drive two screws into each board. Fasten the angles to the stringers using the manufacturer's specified screws (don't use standard deck screws, which are much more vulnerable to shearing off under weight).*

Mount the stringers to the landing with metal framing connectors designed for stair stringers, using the manufacturer's specified fasteners. The outside faces of the stringers should be aligned with the inside faces of the landing posts. Anchor the bottom ends of the stringers to the insides of the starting posts with lag screws and washers.

ADDING THE STEP TREADS

Cut 2 × 6 tread boards to fit snugly between the stringers. The stringers should be perfectly parallel, so you should be able to cut all of the treads at the same length. Each step gets two tread boards. Install each pair of boards starting with the front piece. Align the front edge of the tread with the top edges of the stringers. Fasten the tread with the specified screws driven up through the horizontal flange of the stair angle and into the tread. Each tread gets two screws. Install the second board, leaving a ¼" gap in between for drainage.

BUILDING THE SECOND FLIGHT

The upper section of stairs is constructed almost identically to the first flight, with a couple of minor differences: When cutting and fitting the first stringer, start by making the plumb cut at the top end, matching the angle of the top plumb cuts on the first-flight stringers. Test-fit this cut, and make any necessary adjustments, then trace along the landing to mark the bottom plumb cut.

When laying out the steps, the bottom tread should be 7⅛" higher (measuring vertically) than the top corner of the bottom plumb cut on the stringers. Anchor the stringers to the treehouse platform and the landing with the same stringer connectors used on the first flight. The tops of the stringers should be flush with the tops of the landing and treehouse platform, respectively.

Install a 4 × 4 railing post at the outside of each stringer at the top of the stairs to support the staircase railings.

ADDING THE RAILINGS

For short flights of stairs, you might be fine with 2 × 4 railings spanning between the landing posts and the starting or treehouse railing posts. For longer runs, install mid-span support posts onto the outside faces of the stringers.

Cut the ends of the railings with plumb cuts so they're flush with the faces of the posts. Install the top railings so their top edges are 34" to 36" above the tops of the treads, measuring vertically. Fasten the railings to the inside faces of the posts with long deck screws. Install the bottom railings about halfway between the top railings and the stringers, or you can have three evenly spaced railings on each side. If toddlers will use the stairs, you might want to include vertical balusters spaced just under 4" apart. In any case, both sides of the staircase must have a railing.

Secure the two open sides of the landing with a standard code-compliant railing that matches the railing on the treehouse platform.

Trap Doors

Climbing ropes, secret ladders, and other cool modes of access need an equally cool point of entry: a trap door, of course. The classic trap door is square, with a frame built into the floor joists, and the door itself made from a cutout of the floor boards. Using this basic design you can come up with your own variations—triangular, hexagonal...practically any shape you wish.

To build a trap door, first decide on the size of the opening. With floor joists framed at 24" on center, you're already halfway to making a 22½" square opening. Just add two side pieces between the joists, and the frame is done. With 16" joist spacing, the joists are only 14½" apart—a little too tight for most trap doors. To make a larger opening, cut out the joist running through the planned opening and install two joist headers to carry the cut ends. Then install one or two side pieces between the headers to complete the framed opening. Use the same lumber for the frame as you used for the joists.

Next, add a 1 × 2 stop at each side of the frame, flush with the underside of the floor. Cut out the floor boards flush with the frame pieces (not the stops). Fasten the boards together with 1× cleats or a square of plywood to create the door. Maintain the original spacing between the floor boards so the trap door will blend with the rest of the floor. Mount the door with hinges installed on the back edge of the door so only the barrels of the hinges stick up above the floor. For a handle, cut a finger hole in the door, or install a recessed cabinet pull.

Joist headers support the ends of the cut joist and become two sides of the door opening frame.

A trap door is a fun, secret entry to a treehouse, but it offers some structural advantages as well. For example, if you employ a trap door as your only point of entry you can encircle the treehouse completely with railings.

Fireman's Pole

There's nothing better than a fireman's pole for speedy exits. All it takes to build one is a length of plastic pipe, some concrete, and a piece of plywood or lumber. In a firehouse, firefighters zip down a pole through a large, round opening, but you can set yours up through a square trap door—just cut a slot in the door to fit over the pole when closed.

To make a fireman's pole, cut a length of 3" diameter PVC plumbing pipe to extend from an anchor point on the treehouse down to a foot or so below the ground level. Secure the pole at the top with a ¾" plywood or lumber collar with a hole drilled through it that just fits over the pole. Fasten the collar to the roof framing or other support members. With the bottom of the pole on the ground, the top end should extend about 18" above the collar. Position the pole so it's perfectly plumb, then mark where the pole hits the ground. Dig a 12"-diameter × 12"-deep hole centered around the pole mark. Set the pole in the hole and fill the hole with concrete. Check the pole again for plumb and let the concrete dry.

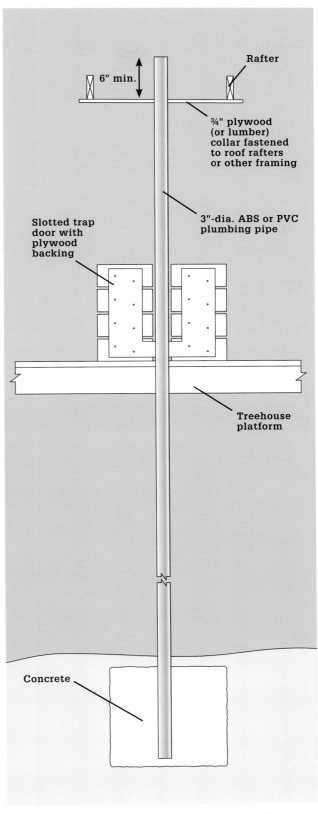

A length of plastic plumbing pipe makes a great fireman's pole. A slotted trap door closes up the access opening.

Swings & Playthings

If you came to this chapter first, you're in the right state of mind for owning a treehouse. If you've just finished your treehouse and are wanting to jazz it up a little, congratulations (you're way ahead of the other guy). One thing that most new treehouse owners learn right away is how much their creation becomes a hub of activity. Kids not only play in treehouses, they play under them and around them and, sometimes, when no one's watching, over them. So it makes sense to add a few extra things for kids to do at the treehouse site. And for the adults? This author recommends a hammock. Period.

A few treehouse accessories are easy to make yourself, like climbing ropes and simple swings. Other add-ons are better purchased from reputable retailers. "Reputable" isn't used lightly, either; you don't want

a zip line manufactured from shoddy materials, for example. Since there's no place to shop for treehouse accessories at your local mall, you'll have to be a little resourceful. The best place to start is with an online search under "play structures," "playground equipment," etc., or with keywords for specific items, such as "climbing walls" or "hammocks." A lot of equipment made for play structures can easily be adapted for a treehouse play area.

A reminder about ground covers: While many of us grew up playing on blacktop playgrounds and sports fields that felt like rammed earth, things are different now. Covering a play area with a thick layer of wood chips or other shock-absorbing material is an easy, effective way prevent injury to kids. It's really a no-brainer, as in no one gets brained from a minor fall.

Swing through the air with the greatest of ease! A tree swing can hang from any suitable limb or a stout treehouse beam, but the connecting point should be at least 10 ft. above the ground for a nice ride (swings for small children can be lower).

Classic Tree Swings

For most people, the love of swinging starts sometime in the first year of life and ends when you realize they just make you too dizzy. We love swings because they make us feel, if only for a brief but repeatable moment, like we're flying. Homemade tree swings are the best, because you can hang them from a tall limb for a long, swooping flight, and you can make them big enough and strong enough for adults.

The two swings shown here are easy to make and equally fun to use, yet each offers a different feel in both the ride and the seating. This is good news, as you'll likely discover that one swing just isn't enough. *Note: To prevent damage to the tree, inspect the rope or hardware connections periodically. You may have to move and/or retie rope connections occasionally if the bark becomes worn or the knot is strangling the limb.*

Choose braided Dacron (polyester) or nylon rope for swings. Twisted rope tends to be too slippery for a good handhold, while polypropylene breaks down in sunlight and manila (though strong) is prone to rotting.

Plank Swing. A traditional plank swing is a good choice for kids of all ages and for adults who prefer a ride that's a little more leisurely than a single-rope button swing. The plank seat is nothing more than a sturdy board with four holes, and no special hardware is needed. The only requirement is a relatively level tree limb to ensure that the swing travels in a straight line. The limited sideways travel on a plank swing makes it the best type for hanging from treehouses or where a tree limb doesn't extend far from the trunk.

CREATING THE SEAT

You can cut and shape the swing seat from almost any nice piece of lumber, such as a treated or cedar 2 × 8. A 1"-thick piece of solid oak or maple makes an especially nice, classic seat. The size is up to you. A standard size is about 6½" to 9¼" wide and 24" to 30" long for a single rider, or larger for a two-seater. Cut the seat to length, rounding the corners with a jigsaw, if desired. Use coarse sandpaper or a router and roundover bit to ease all of the edges of the plank to remove sharpness and prevent splinters.

Lay out and drill four holes through the seat that match the diameter of the swing ropes (⅝"- or ¾"-diameter braided rope is good for plank swings). Center the holes about 1½" to 2" from the ends and side edges of the plank, taking care to lay them out as evenly and symmetrically as possible. Sand the plank smooth, working up to 220-grit sandpaper, then apply exterior-grade polyurethane, exterior paint, or another suitable exterior finish, as directed.

When sizing the plank seat, keep in mind that the usable portion of the seat is limited to the clear area between the rope holes.

A running double bowline setup wraps around the tree limb. It cinches tight when pulled but expands easily as the limb grows in diameter.

Use eye bolts to tie ropes to a treehouse beam or tree limb. Run the bolts up through the center of the beam or limb, and secure the top ends with large washers and locknuts.

TYING TO THE TREE

You can use a number of different knots to secure each rope end to the tree. A swing hitch is one reliable standard. Another is the double bowline knot in a running configuration, a legitimate version of a simple lasso setup. The advantages of the running bowline are that you can tie it off without having to reach the limb, and it expands with the tree's growth without affecting the knot's strength (see How to Tie a Double Bowline Knot, page 140).

You'll need two lengths of rope with plenty of extra for tying off at both ends. Tie one end of each rope to a level section of limb, spacing them the same distance as the hole pairs on the swing seat. Once each rope is secure, hang from the rope with your full weight, to test the knot and take out any initial stretch in the line. The ropes should hang straight down and extend onto the ground at least 2 feet.

How to Tie a Double Bowline Knot ▸

Step 1: Form two loops in the rope, then run the working loose end under and up through the middle of both loops.

Step 2: Run the working end behind and around the standing section of rope.

Step 3: Insert the working end down through both loops.

Step 4: Tighten the knot by holding the working end in place while pulling up on the standing portion, creating a loop near the working end of the rope.

Run the ropes underneath the seat plank and tie them off to themselves several inches above the seat. The triangular formation helps stabilize the seat to prevent tipping.

TYING ON THE SWING SEAT

Holding the seat plank with its top (better) face up, run the rope down through a hole on each end of the plank, then up through the neighboring hole in each pair. Position the plank so it is level and at the desired height from the ground, based on the smallest swinger. Then, tie off the loose end of each rope to the standing section, using a bowline knot (see How to Tie a Bowline Knot, on page 56). Adjust the knots as needed so that the swing seat is level, and give it a test ride. When all looks good, trim the ends of the ropes, if necessary, then melt the ends with the flame of a lighter or match, to prevent unraveling.

Button Swing. Because it hangs from just one rope, a button swing (or disc swing) can tie to almost any strong tree limb, whether it's level or not. A single rope also means you can swing in any direction and can spin until your eyes are crossed. This makes the button not only versatile but a little more adventurous than a plank-style swing. It can be difficult for kids younger than four or five, depending on their arm strength, but they're really fun for bigger kids and adults, especially if the swing hangs from a high limb for a long, sweeping arc.

MARKING THE SEAT

The best way to make a perfectly round seat with a clean edge is by using a router and a simple homemade jig called a trammel. You can also cut the shape with a jigsaw, either freehand or using a trammel. A good standard size for the seat is about 12" in diameter. Suitable materials include ¾" exterior (or marine) plywood, solid 1× lumber, or a piece of redwood or cedar 2 × 12 (with a 1 × 12 or 2 × 12, the maximum diameter will be around 11¼", which is fine).

Whichever cutting technique you're using, the first step is to mark the centerpoint of the seat at least 6" from the nearest edge of the material (for a 12"-diameter disc). To draw the outline of the disc, cut a small notch in the end of a wood slat or yardstick, then drill a small hole for a pivot nail at 6" from the bottom of the notch. Tap a small finish nail into the hole and then into the centerpoint of the workpiece to pin the slat in place. Place the point of a pencil in the notch, and rotate the slat around the nail to draw the circle.

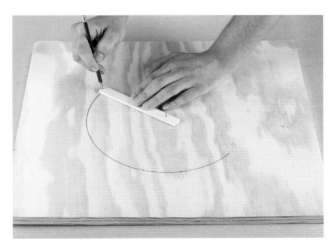

Mark the circular cutting line of the disc using a homemade compass.

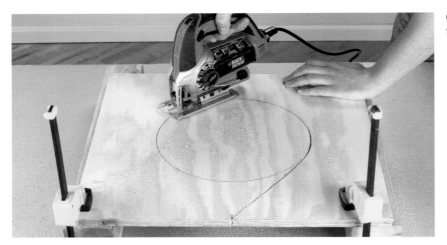

Cut the circle with a jigsaw or trammel-guided router.

Round the edges of the disc with a router or sandpaper for a comfortable ride and to help prevent splinters.

CUTTING THE SEAT

Cut out the disc along the outline, using your preferred method. If you're using a router and trammel, it's a good idea to rough-cut the shape first with a jigsaw (preferably) or a circular saw, staying about ⅛" outside of the cutting line. Then clean up the cut with the router. Cutting off most of the waste saves considerable wear on expensive router bits.

A trammel is essentially a large version of the wood-slat compass, with the router (instead of a pencil) fixed to the outside end. To make a trammel, cut a strip of hardboard or thin plywood to roughly the same width as your router's base. Drill a clearance hole through the board for the router bit, and fasten the trammel to the base with machine bolts set into countersunk pilot holes (you usually have to remove the router's plastic baseplate first). Nail the trammel to the workpiece centerpoint, as with the compass, and rotate the router around the disc to complete the cut. It's best to make the cut in several passes of about ⅛" deep each.

To cut out the disc with a jigsaw, simply do it freehand or attach the saw's foot (base) to a trammel with double-stick tape. Once the disc is cut, smooth any rough spots or saw marks with a router or coarse sandpaper and a sanding block.

COMPLETING THE SEAT

Drill a hole for the rope through the center of the disc, using the finish nail hole to pilot the bit. The hole should be just big enough for threading the rope through. A good choice of rope for a button swing is ⅝" or ¾" braided nylon or Dacron. Nylon is more likely to stretch than Dacron but may be easier to find. Either type should have a working load of at least several hundred pounds.

Round the outside edges on both sides of the disc, using a router and roundover bit or sandpaper. Round the edges of the rope hole slightly to prevent unnecessary wear on the rope. Sand all surfaces of the disc smooth, then apply exterior-grade polyurethane or other exterior finish.

HANGING THE SWING

Tie the rope to a stout tree limb using a swing hitch, a running double bowline knot (see page 140), or other appropriate knot, or use an eye bolt to attach to a treehouse beam, as shown on page 139. Make sure the swing will have plenty of clearance from the tree trunk and other obstructions, keeping in mind the universal travel of the swing.

Hang on the rope to take out any initial slack or stretch. Thread the loose end of the rope through the hole in the disc, and tie off the end underneath the disc with an Ashley Stopper Knot, as shown below. Created by the famed knotsman, Clifford Ashley, the knot has a broad flat top that's perfect for button swings. Melt the cut end of the rope with a lighter or match to prevent fraying.

How to Tie an Ashley Stopper Knot ▶

Step 1: Create a single loop near the working (loose) end of the rope, then run the working end through the loop, creating a second loop.

Step 2: Pull the first loop up through the second loop.

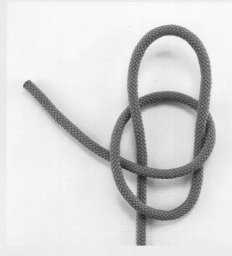

Step 3: Run the working end over the first loop and then under itself, so it's at the back of the knot.

Step 4: Feed the working end through the back of the first loop. Pull the working end and standing portion of the rope to tighten the knot. "Dress" the knot so it is compact and forms a flat surface opposite the working end.

Zip Line

A zip line is a simple contraption consisting of a seat or handle hanging from a heavy-duty pulley that is suspended from a steel cable. The cable is tied between a pair of trees, posts, or other sturdy structures you can find or build—as long as one is higher than the other. If you're starting the cable from a treehouse or platform, make sure any framing that the eyebolt attaches to is rock solid.

A zip line can be slow, gentle, and close enough to the ground to push off and stop yourself with your feet. Or, it can be very high and very fast, carrying you down mountainsides or across lakes, rivers, and canyons. The longest known zip line is 1.2 miles, drops almost 1,000 feet, and reaches speeds of up to 100 miles per hour. These "extreme" zip lines should be created by professionals only and used under the supervision of a qualified professional.

You can create a smaller, safer version of that mind-bending ride in your own backyard with a length of steel cable, some long eyebolts, and a zip line kit

Heavy-duty, exterior-rated eyebolts, washers & nuts	¾" turnbuckle
	Mulch
	Rubber mallet
(2) Metal thimbles for cable	Drill with spade bits & bit extender
(6) Stainless steel cable clamps	Zip line kit
	Eye & ear protection
Discarded tire	Work gloves

with a heavy-duty tandem pulley. Do not use the standard pulleys sold at hardware stores for zip lines—they're not meant for this application. Similarly, use only braided cable (usually stainless steel) that has been specifically selected and packaged for a zip line. You'll find a number of purveyors of zip line products on the Internet (see Resources, page 220).

A zip line is a braided metal cable stretched from a point of access to a point of lower elevation. Add a pulley and a tow bar or handlebars and let the joy rides start.

Safety Tip ▶

Minimum safety equipment when using a zip line includes a harness and helmet. Use other safety equipment (shoulder- and knee-pads, etc.) as required.

A kit and a few basic tools are all you need to install a zip line. Be sure to buy heavy-duty stainless steel or galvanized fittings (kits are available from online suppliers).

Zip Line Requirements ▸

For a good ride, make the zip line at least 75 ft. long, with a minimum slope of five feet. Trees must be heathy and at least 10" in diameter. If you're starting at a treehouse or platform, reinforce the framing with additional fasteners or metal brackets.

Test the run before drilling the holes. Wrap the cable around the trees, secure it with cable clamps and hold it in position at the level where the eyebolt will be attached with wood clamps or large nails. Then tie a heavy sandbag to the handle so it's hanging where a person would be and send it down the cable. If it seems too slow or fast, move one end of the cable to compensate. Watch for obstacles in the path of the cable, and cut branches back four feet on all sides.

Lighter-duty zipline kits made for use by children are sold in relatively inexpensive kits. Their maximum distances traveled range from 30 to 90 ft.

A high-adventure zip line requires a very unusual backyard with tall trees and ample space, as shown here. But setting up a slightly tamer run from your deck to the old maple tree is a great way for active people of all ages to learn and develop skills.

How to Install a Zip Line

Drill a hole through the center of each tree (high end and low end) for an eyebolt. The holes should be the same diameter as the eyebolt shaft. You'll need to use an extra-long spade bit or a bit extender to clear a tree trunk, which should be at least 10" in diameter.

Insert an eyebolt (stainless steel or triple-dipped galvanized) through the guide hole and then secure it to the tree with a wide washer, such as a fender washer, and a nut. The end of the bolt (inset) should protrude 1 to 2" past the tree. Inspect the nut periodically to make sure it is still tight.

Attach a turnbuckle to the eyebolt on the low end of the cable run. The turnbuckle should be sized and rated for the cable size, the total span and the maximum weight load of your zip line.

Loop the cable (use only braided, stainless steel cable rated for zip line usage) through the eyebolt, place a metal thimble at the loop, then secure it in place with three cable clamps.

Thread the loose end of the cable through a non-steel-belted car tire to serve as a safety bumper at the low end of the run. Drill two holes to pass the cable through the center of the tire, then drill several holes in the bottom of the tire for drainage. An alternative option is to install a bungee brake sold by zip line suppliers.

Secure the cable to the turnbuckle at the low end. The turnbuckle should be loosened almost all the way so you can tighten the cable. Pull the cable through the turnbuckle as tightly as you can, and then lock it in place with three cable clamps. Test the tension in the cable, and tighten the turnbuckle as needed.

Clip the handle or trolley onto the cable according to the manufacturer's instructions and test out the zip line, taking care to follow all safety precautions.

Zip lines and launching platforms are perfect additions to treehouses, provided the proper safety equipment is available. Launching platforms should not be considered play areas, and the launching platform should be almost fully enclosed by a 36" code-compliant railing and balusters.

ZIP LINE PLATFORMS

Zip lines need an elevated platform for starting the ride. A treehouse can be ideal for this, offering plenty of elevation for most zip lines, as well as a nice, solid base for launching. Perhaps most importantly, if you're up in the treehouse having fun when Mom calls you in for dinner or bedtime, at least you can end your play on a high note, with a triumphant last ride down the zip line. Sure beats trudging down the ladder grumbling about how unfair it is that you have to eat and sleep.

If it isn't feasible to use your treehouse as a launching platform, you can simply build a standalone platform designed specifically for this purpose. This can be quite small—say, 3 × 3 feet—and can hang from a tree or from one or more support posts.

In any case, it's important to note that a launching platform should not be designed or used as a general play area. For one thing, it has a fairly large opening without a safety railing, and second, the rider should not be distracted as he prepares for the launch, lest he forget to grip the trolley bar with both hands, for example. The first rule of the launching platform must be: One person at a time on the platform. With a group of kids crowding around itching to take a ride, one can only imagine the kinds of hazards they might invent.

BUILDING A STANDALONE PLATFORM

A standalone launching platform can employ any of the platform design elements and anchoring techniques discussed in the treehouse building techniques section (pages 60–83). A simple version uses a saddle design in which the platform joists anchor to either side of the tree, with two knee braces doing the same a few feet below.

Depending on the size of the host tree, the platform deck can be around 3 to 4 feet wide and 3 to 4 feet deep. It should have a 36"-high railing on the sides, with balusters spaced just under 4" apart. The weight loads are pretty minimal here, so a 2 × 6 frame with a 2 × 4 railing is suitable for a small platform like this.

For access to the platform, a permanently attached ladder, such as the double-rung and flat-rung styles shown on pages 126 through 128, is a good option that's relatively easy to build. The access ladder should approach from the side and include a safety rail across the top of the opening. The height of the platform is up to you, but it must provide a sufficient drop in elevation for a good ride; a good rule-of-thumb dictates at least a 75-foot run and a 5-foot drop in elevation.

Launching from a Treehouse ▸

With the right setup, any open-deck portion of a treehouse can be designed or adapted to serve as a launching area, but there are a few important factors to consider. First, there must be a clear path for travel along the line; you don't want the cable crossing over traffic routes or common areas of the treehouse. Second, the cable's anchor point should be within 3 to 4 feet of the drop-off edge of the platform. The cable's sag is most pronounced at the beginning of the run; if the anchor point is too far back, the rider might bump along the platform on the way out. Finally, the platform should be separated from the common/play areas of the treehouse. This is best achieved with a latched safety gate that bars access to little kids and helps older kids adhere to the "one person at a time" rule.

Often, the best plan is to locate the launching platform in a relatively remote part of the treehouse structure, such as behind the house or at the far corner of a deck. Another option is to add a bump-out onto the main platform or deck area using cantilevered joists or additional knee braces and other support members as needed. It is important that the path is clear along the route of the line, that the cable's anchor point is within 3 to 4 feet of the edge of the platform, and that the platform be separated from the common area of the treehouse with a safety gate or other barrier.

Rock Climbing Wall

There seems to be something Darwinian in a kid's innate desire and ability to climb. And they'll use anything to "get off the deck," as rock climbers say. This makes a climbing wall a good bet for a treehouse accessory. Climbing walls build muscles and confidence and are probably the most fun of all modes of access for getting up into a treehouse.

A climbing wall is easy to build, but it takes the right equipment to make sure it's safe, versatile, and suitable for the resident climbers. While the wall structure is a simple assembly of framing lumber and painted plywood, the holds—the roughly textured, contoured pieces used for climbing—should be chosen carefully to accommodate the climbers' ages and abilities. Rock climbing equipment manufacturers make this easy by offering a variety of sets of holds in a range of sizes and shapes.

The climbing holds are secured to the wall with bolts and T-nuts, which affix themselves to the backside of the plywood, so they're always there when it's time to change the climbing route. Therein lies the unique benefit of climbing walls: You can easily rearrange the holds to create new routes at any time. The wall's versatility depends on a few factors: the overall size of the wall, the number of holes (and T-nuts) in the plywood, and the number of holds you have to work with.

For toddlers and elementary-school-aged climbers, plan to purchase about 32 holds per 4 × 8-foot section of wall. Older climbers can do well with fewer holds—about 18 to 24 holds per 4 × 8-foot section. It's well worth it to buy a good set up front to make the wall both versatile and fun to use. A set of 32 holds with hardware costs around $80 to $120. It's also recommended that you buy from a legitimate rock climbing gear supplier, rather than a toy company, which might have cheap plastic holds that aren't sturdy and don't simulate the feel of real rock.

Rock walls are great skill-builders for climbers of any age. With a sizeable wall and plenty of holds, you have the flexibility to change the routes periodically to keep things interesting and challenging.

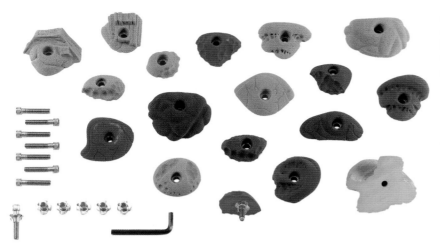

A **variety pack of holds**—with plenty of medium- and large-size pieces—is ideal for a treehouse rock wall. Make sure the holds and all hardware are rated for outdoor use.

FRAMING THE WALL

To build a simple vertical wall that's attached to the ground at the bottom and the treehouse structure at the top, start by constructing a 2 × 4 frame sized to match the overall dimensions of the wall. Cut the outside studs the full length of the wall minus 3", then cut a top and bottom plate to fasten to the studs. Assemble the frame with 3" deck screws or 16d galvanized common nails. Install interior studs between the plates, spacing them 16" on center. If the wall is wider than one 4 × 8 sheet of plywood, make sure there's a stud centered behind every plywood seam.

TEXTURING THE SURFACE

Prime each panel of ¾" exterior-grade plywood on all surfaces, using an exterior-grade primer. Paint the front faces of the panels (which should be the "A," or better, side) with exterior house paint mixed with a texture material, or use non-slip flooring paint. Creating a textured surface offers several advantages: it makes the wall surface less slippery, to facilitate climbing; it helps to prevent the holds from turning under force—a common problem with some single-bolt holds; and, perhaps most importantly, it keeps the holds from sticking to the paint.

You can create the textured surface by simply adding a texture material, such as SharkGrip, to exterior house paint, or use an exterior flooring paint designed for patios and pool surrounds, such as Floor-Tex. Apply the products following the manufacturer's directions. Paint the edges and back faces of the panels with ordinary exterior house paint.

Build the wall frame with pressure-treated 2 × 4s. Large or freestanding walls might require larger framing members.

A texture additive turns ordinary house paint into a highly workable texture paint. Lightweight, low-density materials, such as polymer beads, are easy to work with because they remain suspended in the paint; sand and other heavy materials tend to sink, requiring frequent mixing.

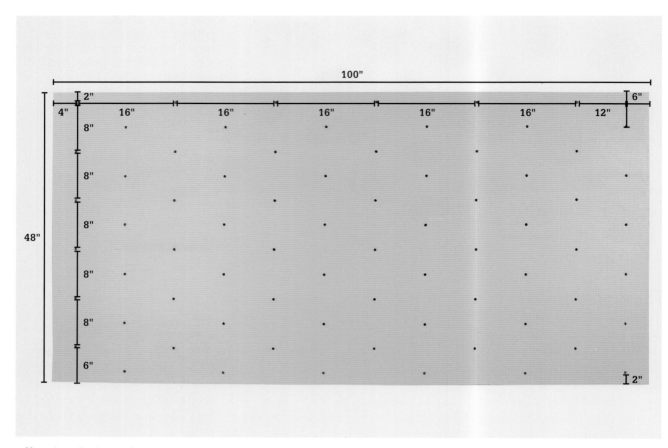

Offsetting the holes for the climbing holds by 4" between rows gives you the best distribution over the wall area. Keeping the holes 2" from the side edges ensures the T-nuts will be clear of the wall framing.

Hammer the T-nuts into back of the wall panel(s).
Make sure that the nuts are perfectly flat so that the threaded sleeves are properly aligned for the bolts.

DRILLING THE HARDWARE HOLES

Lay out the hole pattern onto the front faces of the panel(s), as shown here. A full 4 × 8-foot panel gets 72 holes. Drill each hole with a 7⁄16" spade or twist bit, keeping the bit straight and drilling from the front face of the panel to prevent tearout on the exposed surface. If desired, prime and/or paint the hole interiors for added moisture protection.

INSTALLING THE T-NUTS

Install the T-nuts onto the back face of the panel(s), using a hammer. Center each nut over a hole, with the nut's sleeve facing into the hole. Carefully hammer the nut, driving the pointed tips into the plywood, until the rear flange of the nut is flush with the plywood surface. Every hole in the panel(s) should get a nut. *Note: To prevent corrosion, be sure to use exterior-grade nuts and bolts. Most climbing wall suppliers offer stainless steel bolts and zinc-plated T-nuts—a good combination for long-term strength and corrosion resistance.*

COMPLETING THE WALL

Fasten the panel(s) to the 2 × 4 frame with 1⅝"
deck screws driven every 6" along the edges and
every 8" in the field of the sheet. Countersink
the screw heads slightly below the surface of the
plywood. If the wood splinters around the heads,
drill countersunk pilot holes for the screws. To
automatically square up the frame as you work,
start at one corner of the wall, aligning the plywood
with the two adjacent edges of the frame. If you're
using more than one panel, make sure the joints
between panels are tight and flush, with no gaps or
raised edges.

To install the wall onto the treehouse, first dig a
small trench under the wall location, about 4" deep.
Fill the trench with gravel, then level and compact
it firmly. Cut a base from a pressure-treated 4 × 4
to match the width of the wall. Drill three ⅜" holes
through the base. Level the base atop the gravel.
Measure to confirm that the wall will be flush with or
slightly below the top of the treehouse platform when
installed. Anchor the base to the ground with 12"
lengths of #4 rebar.

Set the wall on top of the base. Anchor the top
end of the wall to the platform structure with ⅜"
carriage bolts or machine bolts and washers. The bolt
heads should be on the front face of the wall and
should be countersunk into the wood if they're not
rounded. Fasten the bottom end of the wall to the
4 × 4 base with 4" lag screws.

Arrange the holds as desired, securing them to
the T-nuts with ⅜" stainless steel bolts (most have
Allen heads). Torque the bolts as specified by the
hold manufacturer.

Bolt the holds to the wall, making sure they're tight and properly positioned. Now it's time to crank.

Water Cannon

This is without question the most fun you can have with pressurized water. And after putting in a number of weekends on the treehouse itself, you'll be glad to know that you can easily create this cannon in an hour, using parts that cost less than $15 at your local home center. That means you can start the project during the cool hours of a summer morning and have the cannon installed and ready for battle in the midday heat.

The cannon shown here is made with ¾" PVC pipe and fittings. All of the unthreaded connections are glued with PVC cement (solvent glue). If you're handy with a torch, you could create a similar version using copper pipe. Once assembled, the cannon mounts onto a swiveling caster screwed into a post or the top of a treehouse railing.

The nozzle at the end of the cannon barrel is an ordinary straight-style garden nozzle, the type that you twist to turn on the water and adjust the spray. In this case, it's best to leave the nozzle open and use the ball valve located on the cannon's handle to control the water flow. Nozzles are available in a few different styles. Standard twist types offer the most adjustment capability and plenty of power at full concentration, while jet-style nozzles deliver a highly concentrated stream and the longest range (but this might be overkill for most applications).

Man the ramparts (and water the lawn while you're at it)! This water cannon has its own shutoff valve and nozzle control, so you'll never have to leave the castle unguarded to reload or retool.

A coil-type garden hose provides the best maneuverability at the cannon end of the water line. You can attach a short coil hose to a standard garden hose, leaving plenty of slack in the coil for easy movement.

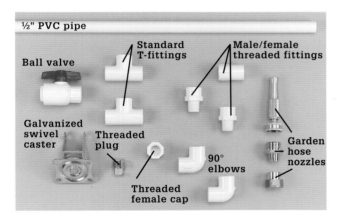

The cannon is as easy to build as it is fun to use.

ASSEMBLING THE CANNON

To build the cannon, cut two lengths of pipe at 11" and 6" for the long and short barrel pieces. Cut the pipe with a hacksaw, tubing cutter, or miter saw. A jigsaw with a fine-tooth blade works well, too. Clean the cut ends. Onto one end of the long barrel piece, prime and solvent-glue a pipe to hose fitting with a ½" male threaded end.

Buying the Parts ▸

A well-stocked home center or hardware store should have all of the parts you need, but plan to spend a few minutes in the plumbing section sorting through the various boxes for the right fittings. Here are the supplies needed to build the cannon as shown; all parts are for ¾" PVC pipe:

36 linear inches of ¾" pipe
1 — T fitting with threaded down tube
1 — threaded plug (threaded end must be enclosed)
1 — T fitting (standard; all unthreaded tubes)
2 — 90-degree elbow fittings
2 — pipe to male threaded fittings
1 — PVC ball valve with female threaded ends
1 — pipe to hose fitting (¾" male threaded end; female threaded end for standard ½" hose)
1 — threaded (female) cap
1 — pipe to hose fitting (¾" unthreaded female end; male threaded end for standard ½" hose end)
PVC primer
PVC cement (schedule 40)
1 — galvanized swivel caster with 1⅞" or 2" wheel (need at least 1⅛" of space for wheel width, to accommodate T fitting)
1 — garden hose nozzle

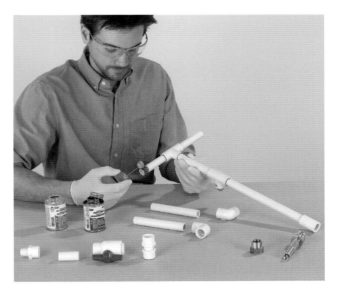

Solvent-gluing plastic pipe is easy: Brush primer onto the mating parts, then brush on the cement. Quickly fit the pieces together, giving them a ¼-turn to spread the glue, and hold firmly for 30 seconds. The directions on the can tell you exactly what to do—just be sure to follow them carefully.

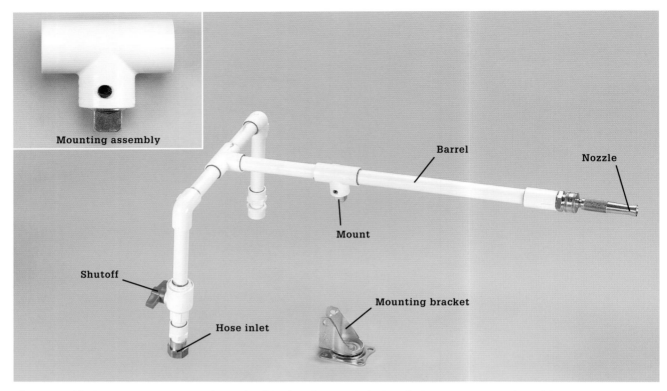

The assembled cannon. You can set the angle of the handles to suit the installation and the gunner's position. Drill the hole for the caster axle bolt (inset), making sure the upper portion of the plug will maintain a watertight seal.

Glue the other end of the long barrel to a T fitting with a threaded down tube, then glue the short barrel to the opposite unthreaded tube of the T. The threaded tube end of the T is where the cannon mounts to the caster, via a hole you will drill through the T. To prevent water from escaping through the T and the hole, cap off the T end with a threaded male plug glued in place and threaded in as far as possible.

Next, glue a standard T to the bare end of the short barrel so the two top tubes are level. Cut two lengths of pipe at 4", and glue these to the T. At the end of each 4" piece, glue an elbow that angles down and back about 20 degrees from vertical, or as desired. To the open ends of the elbows, glue two 5½" lengths of pipe to create the handles. Then, glue on a pipe to male threaded fitting. Set the assembly aside for two hours (or as directed) to let the solvent glue cure.

At this stage, the cannon is perfectly symmetrical, and the remaining fittings are screwed on. This means you can always change which side receives the valve and hose. Onto one of the male threaded ends, screw a PVC ball valve, followed by a threaded pipe to hose fitting (½" male end screws into valve; ¾" female end receives garden hose). On the other handle's fitting, screw a threaded cap. You can remove this cap to drain the handle, as desired. To facilitate tightening and prevent leaks, use Teflon tape for all threaded connections (except the glued plug on the barrel T).

INSTALLING THE CANNON

To mount the cannon, remove the wheel from the caster's axle bolt. Carefully drill a hole through the T on the cannon barrel, drilling all the way through the fitting and plug and keeping the hole close to the bottom end of the T—you want to leave plenty of threaded area to ensure a watertight seal above the hole. The hole should be just large enough to fit the axle bolt. Fasten the caster upside down onto the treehouse railing, a post, or other anchor point, using deck screws. Fit the axle bolt through the caster arms—with the cannon T in the middle—and secure it with the nut.

Attach a coil-type or other garden hose to the handle, and run the water full blast for a few seconds to flush out any plastic debris. Add the nozzle, and you're ready to defend the fortress!

Speaking Tube

For the average treehouse dweller, a speaking tube is a special telephone useful for spies, pirates, and clubhouse top brass. By standard definition, a speaking tube is a 19th-century intercom system that uses pipes to transmit sound over relatively long distances. They were used in Victorian homes to talk with visitors at the front door and to summon servants from distant rooms. And kids will like to know that speaking tubes have long been important for communication on naval ships, where some are still in use today.

You can get a sense of the effectiveness of speaking tubes by whispering back and forth through a long pipe at the home center or through a garden hose at home. Even the slightest murmur can be clearly heard across the longest pipe. This is because sound travels on air, which is channeled through the pipe directly from the speaker to the listener, without being dispersed and dissipating into the open.

Constructing a speaking tube is very simple, and you can use a variety of pipe or tube materials—really anything that moves air efficiently. Here, you'll see how to install an underground speaking tube made of PVC pipe and learn about a vertical version made with copper pipe. PVC pipe also works just as well as copper for an aboveground tube. For long underground runs, you might prefer to use flexible PE tubing for the underground portion and construct the exposed ends with rigid PVC or copper pipe and fittings. Whatever tubing you use, it's a good idea to test out the material and the overall tube design before installing or burying any parts.

UNDERGROUND SPEAKING TUBE

Underground tubes seem especially magical because you don't see any of the tubing connecting the visible talking/listening uprights at the ends. The buried piping can run under an entire play area and make turns as needed along the way. An underground tube can also be connected to a vertical tube to send messages between a treehouse and a point on the ground some distance away.

PLANNING THE PIPE ROUTE

A speaking tube can work well at 50 yards or even farther between the ends. That's probably a lot more than you need—especially when you consider that an underground tube requires trenching. But it's useful information if you're planning to make long distance

A **speaking tube** is a fail-safe communication device for transmitting top-secret information or fresh knock-knock jokes. You may have tried one of these at a public playground, but your own version is likely to work much better.

calls. The important thing is to test the system before digging the trench. Fortunately, PVC pipe is cheap enough that you can buy a couple of extra lengths to test a longer tube, even if you end up not using it.

To plan your tube route, lay out lengths of 1" rigid PVC pipe above the intended underground path, using PVC couplings to join the pieces. Use a 45° or 90° elbow to make turns, as needed. Just keep in mind that the more efficiently the air flows through the pipes, the better the sound will be at the receiving end. Cut the pipes to length as needed, using a tubing cutter, hacksaw, or jigsaw with a fine-tooth blade.

Lay out the underground sections of piping to plan the final route before testing the system.

The end of the tube is made with a PVC reducing fitting. You can embellish this with a larger cone-shaped device, which may enhance the sound somewhat but is not necessary.

ASSEMBLING THE ENDS

Each end of the buried portion of the speaking tube feeds into an upright section that includes the open end for listening or speaking into. These can be any height you like. To create each upright, dry-fit (no glue) a 90° elbow onto the end of the underground pipe so the open end of the elbow is pointing straight up. Add a vertical section of pipe, followed by another 90° elbow and a 1½" or larger reducer fitting. The reducer serves as the mouthpiece, the equivalent of the cone-shaped "trumpet" end found on traditional speaking tubes.

The uprights should be secured to some kind of rigid structure, such as a tree, a treehouse support post, or a short 4 × 4 post installed for this purpose. Install a short post by setting it into a hole and backfilling around the post with tamped layers of soil and compactible gravel. With both uprights dry-assembled, give the speaking tube a test run.

ASSEMBLING THE PIPE

When all looks good, dig the trench for the underground pipe, and permanently install any support posts for the uprights. Be sure to "call before you dig," so you know for sure there aren't any utility lines in the installation area. Dig the pipe trench about 6" deep in an unsodded play area or 9" to 12" deep under a lawn.

Assemble the underground pipe run using PVC primer and cement (solvent glue), as directed by the manufacturer. The basic gluing process is to brush primer onto the mating parts, then brush on a coating of cement. Quickly fit the pieces together, giving them a twist to spread the glue, and hold the pieces firmly for 30 seconds. Make sure the 90° elbows at the ends of the underground section are pointing straight up.

Lay the completed pipe into the trench. Glue together the pieces of the uprights, starting with the straight pipes leading from the underground elbows and finishing with the reducing fittings. Let the entire pipe assembly rest undisturbed for at least two hours, or as directed.

Join the tube parts with solvent glue. The glue sets up in 30 seconds, but the joints shouldn't be stressed for two hours.

COMPLETING THE TUBE

After the solvent glue has cured, lay the pipe into the trench. Secure the uprights to their supports with metal or plastic pipe straps and deck screws. Backfill the trench with the displaced soil, tamp it flat, and replace the sod or ground cover, as applicable.

Tip: To prevent kids from dropping stuff down into the tube's ends, cut a piece of hardware cloth to fit inside the reducer, securing it with a little caulk or epoxy. Anything dropped into the pipe will reduce the tube's effectiveness, and extricating something valuable requires digging up and cutting into the tubing.

PVC pipe is flexible and strong, but it is breakable. Secure the uprights with pipe straps to prevent any damage.

Vertical Speaking Tube ▸

For many treehouses, a speaking tube going straight up along the tree or support post and into the house is just the thing—ideal for delivering secret passwords for treehouse access or reporting news between the house and the ground (or between the crow's nest and the deck, the control tower and the tarmac, etc.). The vertical tube is crafted with copper pipe and fittings, mostly because copper looks good and because the overall run is short enough to make the cost reasonable. You can build a similar tube less expensively with PVC or other plastic plumbing parts.

A vertical design can follow just about any path, but a more direct route tends to yield better sound quality. Use 45° or 90° elbow fittings to make turns, following the supporting structure. Plan to support the piping every few feet. To run the tube up into the treehouse, drill a ⅞"- or 1"-dia. hole through the platform, using a hole saw or spade bit.

A good size of pipe for a speaking tube is ¾", although larger pipe also works. Cut the straight lengths of pipe for the run, starting at one end of the planned route. Secure the pipe to supports, such as the treehouse framing or support posts, using copper pipe strapping and short deck screws.

To make turns, use elbows and other fittings in the run. For this application, the piping doesn't have to be watertight, so you can glue on the fittings with a small amount of metal epoxy or other adhesive, or solder the joints just enough to hold them together.

Finish each end of the speaking tube with a 90° elbow, a short horizontal pipe, and a reducer fitting, all glued or soldered in place. Any size of reducer will work, but bigger is better; for example, a 2"-to-¾" reducer is a good size that's commonly available.

Slides

As an elevated perch and play structure, a treehouse for young kids pretty much has to have a slide. This leaves you with two options: buying a plastic prefab slide or building your own with lumber and (the secret ingredient) plastic laminate. That's right, the countertop material. But we'll get to those details later.

Prefab slides come in a wide range of sizes and shapes, from straight waves to curlicue "turbo" tubes. They also range widely in price, from sort of pricey to turbo expensive. Large or elaborate models may require assembly, but otherwise all you have to do is anchor the slide at the top and bottom and add a mid-span support, if applicable.

A slide is an ideal accessory for any kids' treehouse that's close to the ground. All slides should have a safety rail that continues the line of the railing across the opening at the top of the slide.

DIY SLIDE

There are a few reasons you might prefer a homemade design. First, DIY slides can be extra slippery and fast. That's what slides are for, right? Many plastic slides create too much friction for a smooth, swift glide. Second, while a homemade slide contains some plastic, it doesn't have to look like a monstrous toy in a glaring primary color, as do most prefab models. The sides are painted redwood, and the slide surface can be any (light) color you choose from your laminate supplier. And finally, you might be tempted to build a slide simply because you can, and because it certainly will be the only one like it on the block.

FITTING THE STRINGERS

The stringers are the two structural sides of the slide, which also create the side walls to prevent sliders from making an early dismount. For a slide that's roughly 8 feet long, 2 × 8 redwood or cedar stringers (at 10 feet long) are a good option. Be sure to use lumber that's smooth on all sides and edges. In terms of grade, "all-heart" redwood will last longer in the weather than lower grades. You'll start by custom-cutting one stringer to fit the installation, then use the cut piece as a pattern to mark and cut the remaining stringer so the two are identical.

Hold one of the stringer boards in place so it spans from the treehouse platform (the launching area) to the ground (the landing area). The standard slope for slides is about 30 degrees, and you can adjust this as desired. The steeper the slope, the faster the

slide. Just keep in mind that this slide doesn't level out at the bottom like most playground slides, so be careful not to make it too fast.

Mark the bottom edge of the board at both ends for the initial cuts to fit them to the platform and ground. You'll probably cut more than once for a good fit. Cut the ends with a circular saw or jigsaw. Test the fit and fine-tune the cuts as needed. The top ends of the stringers are notched to fit over the end of the platform (see photo on 160). The bottom end has a level cut that follows the ground and a plumb end cut that's perpendicular to the level cut.

Shape the top corners of the stringer with 1"-radius roundovers, or as desired. Make the cuts with a jigsaw or handsaw, and sand them smooth. Lay the cut stringer over the remaining board and transfer all of the cuts and roundovers, then cut the remaining stringer.

CREATING THE SLIDE SURFACE

The slide surface is ¾" ACX plywood covered on its top face with plastic laminate (a.k.a. Formica). Laminate sheets are commonly available in widths of 3 to 5 feet and lengths of 6 to 12 feet. For most slides, a 3-foot-wide piece is more than enough. Be sure to choose "standard" laminate designed for countertops; thinner VT (or vertical-grade) laminate isn't as durable. Also be sure to select a light color to reflect heat. A standard textured surface is preferable to a high-gloss surface.

You can build the slide surface in a few different

Position the first stringer board at approximately 30°, and mark the ends for a notch cut at the top and a level cut at the ground.

Glue the laminate to the smooth face of the plywood, using contact cement. Using old mini blind slats or clean wood strips as spacers helps you position the laminate before sticking it down. Once it's fully bonded, trim the laminate flush to the plywood edges.

ways. One is to rough-cut the plywood to size, apply the laminate, then trim the edges of both the plywood and laminate with a saw (cutting from the backside of the plywood). Another is to cut both materials to the finished size before gluing on the laminate. A third method follows the standard process for countertops and other finished surfaces: Cut the plywood to size, apply the laminate so it overhangs all of the plywood edges, then trim the laminate flush to the plywood with a router and flush-trimming bit. This method leaves the most room for error when gluing the laminate, and it's the best way to cut the laminate without chipping the edges.

Cut the plywood to the desired length and width, using a circular saw. It's a good idea to make the finished slide at least 24" wide, to accommodate thrill-seeking adults. Add 1" to the desired width of the slide surface, because ½" of each side edge will be captured in a dado groove in the stringer. Sand the top face of the plywood (the good "A" side) so it is smooth and flat.

Cut the laminate sheet to a manageable size, about 3" longer and wider than the plywood piece, using tin snips, a router, or a circular saw. Apply the laminate with waterproof contact cement, following the manufacturer's directions. After the laminate is stuck, roll it out carefully with a J-roller to strengthen the bond and remove any air bubbles. Trim the excess laminate along the edges of the plywood with the router.

PREPARING THE STRINGERS

Using the router and a roundover bit, round over all exposed edges of each stringer. This is a critical step for safety and to prevent splinters, so if you don't have a router, round over the edges with coarse sandpaper and a sanding block. Don't rout or sand the edges of the dadoes.

Sand all surfaces (except the dadoes) thoroughly, making sure everything is smooth and splinter-free, working up to at least 150-grit sandpaper. Tape off the dadoes, then prime and paint the stringers with quality exterior primer and house paint. It's a shame to hide redwood with a thick coat of paint, but it's necessary to prevent weathering that leads to splinters and cracks.

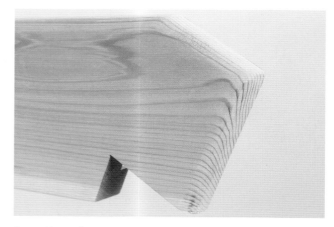

Smooth surfaces are a key safety feature. Rounding the edges of the stringers helps prevent splintering and makes them more comfortable for gripping and gliding.

ASSEMBLING THE SLIDE

The best way to join the slide surface with the stringers is by setting the surface's edges into dadoes, which you can mill with a router or cut with a table saw and a dado blade. If you don't have one of these tools, you can simply use 2 × 2s underneath the slide surface, fastening them to the stringers and plywood with glue and screws.

To mill the dadoes with a router, set up an edge guide on the router base so the bottom of the dado will be 1½" from the bottom edge of each stringer. Mill the dadoes with a straight bit so the finished groove matches the thickness of the slide surface (it will probably be a little over ¾").

Assemble the slide by applying exterior-grade (waterproof) wood glue to the dadoes and fitting the stringers over the sides of the slide surface. Clamp the assembly together, making sure the stringers are perpendicular to the surface. After the glue cures, seal the joints from moisture with fine beads of exterior caulk applied along the corners where the surface meets the stringers.

INSTALLING THE SLIDE

Mount the completed slide to the treehouse platform using galvanized metal brackets or another appropriate anchoring method. Fasten a bracket to each stringer using short carriage bolts or screws, then fasten the brackets to the platform with lag screws or heavy-duty deck screws.

At the bottom end, the slide should be resting on firm, level ground. Add plenty of soft mulch or other suitable groundcover in the slide landing area. Replenish the groundcover as needed to ensure a soft landing.

Dadoed stringers make for the cleanest assembly. Be sure to use waterproof glue (polyurethane glue or exterior-rated wood glue) to permanently bond the slide surface into the stringers.

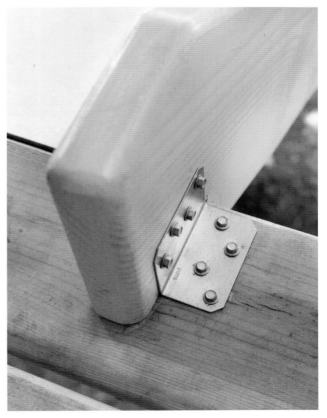

Mount the top ends of the slide stringers to the treehouse with metal brackets and screws (or bolts)—all materials must be corrosion-resistant.

Treehouse Projects

If you've stuck with us from the beginning of the book you've learned how to design and build each part of a treehouse. Now you can see all those parts come together in two start-to-finish treehouse projects completed in real backyards. The designs of the houses are intentionally quite different: One is a lot like a terrestrial house and is built in a single tree; the other is an open-sided affair supported by a large tree and two posts. Of course, these projects just scratch the surface of options and features that you might incorporate into your own design. For a few more ideas, check out the treehouse plans on pages 196–219.

In this chapter:

- Open-air Treehouse
- Gable House with Entry Deck
- Gable Roof with Auxiliary Posts
- A-frame with Walkout Deck
- Half-covered Crow's Nest
- Wraparound Shed on Stilts
- Triangular Tree Hut
- Four-tree Shanty

Open-air Treehouse

This house design could just as easily be called the All-ages Treehouse. Adults will like it because they can move around in the house without having to see their chiropractor the next day and because the broad deck surface and ample headroom make it a great venue for outdoor entertaining and everyday cocktails at sundown. Kids will love it because, well, because it's a treehouse, but also because it's large enough to fit loads of them. The open sides are ideal for backyard games, and the deck makes the perfect stage for picnics and campouts. Best of all, everyone can use the treehouse at once, although this may require a willingness to dodge water balloons or act as a captive on a pirate ship.

The house shown in this project has an 8 × 12-foot floor plan and measures about 9 feet from the deck to the roof peak. It's supported along the front side by two posts and along the rear side by two trees (see page 171), using special anchors designed specifically for treehouses. The treehouse deck stands about 8 feet off the ground.

The instructions here provide a detailed overview of building the house as shown, for this particular site. They can serve as a general guide to help you design and build a similar house of your own. However, all of the construction specifications for your project must be geared for your specific house design, the intended use of the house, the tree(s), and the building site, as well as any applicable local building codes and zoning restrictions.

Water-resistant cushions are ideal for the open-air treehouse, perfect for extra seat padding or just throwing on the ground—it's a treehouse, after all.

The open-air treehouse combines the versatility of an elevated deck with the shelter of a covered porch, but of course it's far better than both because it's found in the trees.

Open-air Treehouse

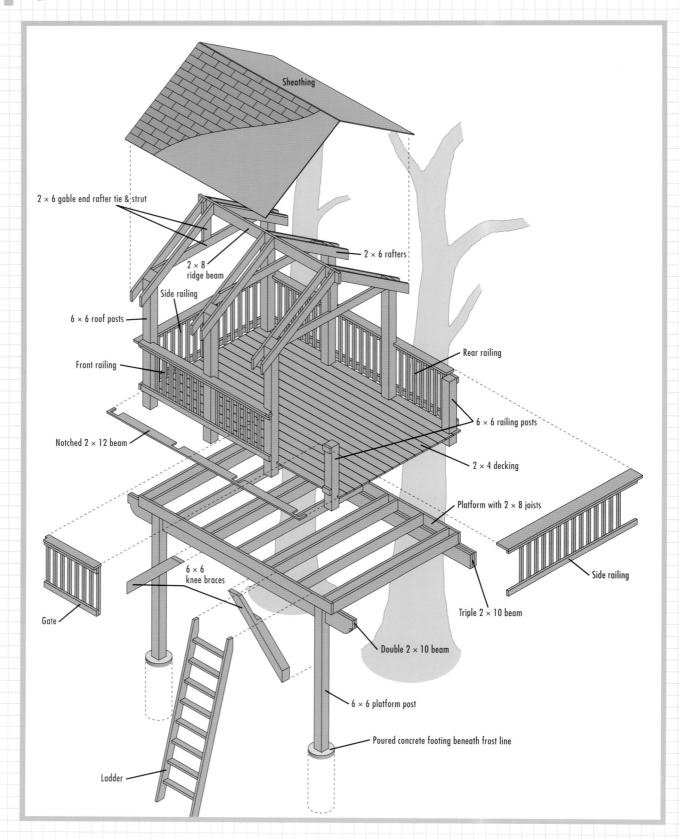

Sheathing

2 × 6 gable end rafter tie & strut

2 × 6 rafters

2 × 8 ridge beam

Side railing

6 × 6 roof posts

Rear railing

Front railing

6 × 6 railing posts

Notched 2 × 12 beam

2 × 4 decking

Platform with 2 × 8 joists

6 × 6 knee braces

Side railing

Gate

Triple 2 × 10 beam

Double 2 × 10 beam

6 × 6 platform post

Poured concrete footing beneath frost line

Ladder

PLAN VIEW: PLATFORM FRAMING

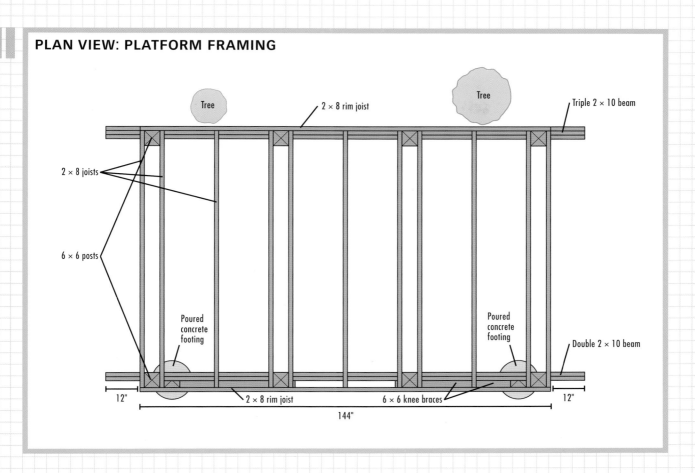

Tree

2 × 8 rim joist

Tree

Triple 2 × 10 beam

2 × 8 joists

6 × 6 posts

Poured concrete footing

Poured concrete footing

Double 2 × 10 beam

12"

2 × 8 rim joist

6 × 6 knee braces

12"

144"

FRONT ELEVATION

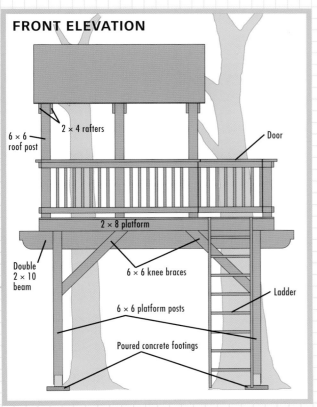

2 × 4 rafters

6 × 6 roof post

Door

2 × 8 platform

Double 2 × 10 beam

6 × 6 knee braces

Ladder

6 × 6 platform posts

Poured concrete footings

SIDE ELEVATION

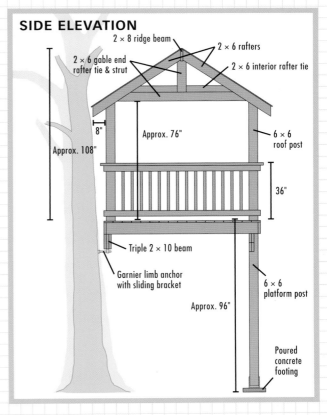

2 × 8 ridge beam

2 × 6 rafters

2 × 6 gable end rafter tie & strut

2 × 6 interior rafter tie

8"

Approx. 76"

6 × 6 roof post

Approx. 108"

36"

Triple 2 × 10 beam

Garnier limb anchor with sliding bracket

6 × 6 platform post

Approx. 96"

Poured concrete footing

DETAIL: LADDER

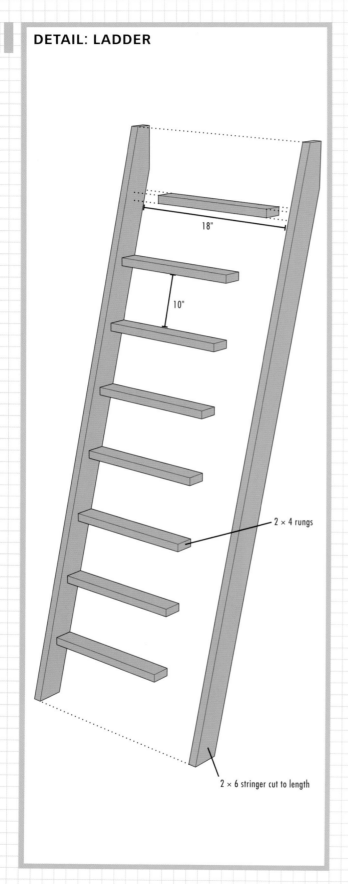

18"

10"

2 × 4 rungs

2 × 6 stringer cut to length

DETAIL: ROOF FRAMING

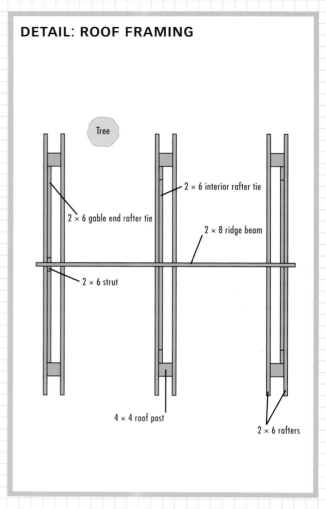

Tree

2 × 6 interior rafter tie

2 × 6 gable end rafter tie

2 × 8 ridge beam

2 × 6 strut

4 × 4 roof post

2 × 6 rafters

DETAIL: CEILING

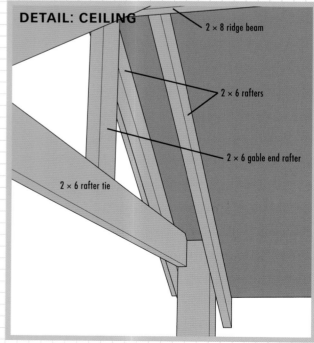

2 × 8 ridge beam

2 × 6 rafters

2 × 6 gable end rafter

2 × 6 rafter tie

LOCATING THE ANCHOR POINTS

This treehouse has four anchor points: one 6 × 6 post at each of the front corners of the platform and one tree anchor near each of the rear corners. The anchors used here are the standard GL anchors (see Resources page 220), which screw directly into the tree and support a structural beam for the treehouse platform. If you use GL or other tree anchors, be sure to follow the supplier's or manufacturer's recommendations for installation and load-bearing capacity. When installed properly, the anchors used here are rated for a load of 4,000 pounds.

Start by locating the anchor points on the host tree (or trees). Mark the trunk or limb at the approximate height of the treehouse deck minus 18" (the combined depth of the treehouse platform and beam). Inspect the tree in this area carefully to make sure it's suitable for an anchor. It must be at least 12" in diameter, and it must be solid and healthy: no rot, fungus, cracks, splits, insect damage, or any other indications of existing or potential weakness.

If the first anchor point gets the go-ahead, level over with a long, straight board to the other tree anchor location. You can use straps or tape to hold the board in place for now; there's no need to put in nails for this procedure. The board also tests how easily you can plane across from one anchor to the next, which you will ultimately do with the beam. Inspect the

second anchor point area, then move to the ground. Measure out from the tree, or more accurately, from the board, and mark the ground at the approximate locations of the two posts. It's best if the ground is relatively level, but most importantly it must be solid and not vulnerable to erosion.

INSTALLING THE TREE ANCHORS

The GL tree anchor requires a precisely made 3-stage pilot hole that accommodates the leading threaded end of the anchor shaft and a short unthreaded portion of the shaft, plus a bore for the collar to bed into the cambium layer of the tree (see page 25 (Treeschool sidebar). If you use this anchor, it's highly recommended that you drill the pilot hole with the special bit designed for this application (it's available for purchase or rent from the supplier; see Resources page 220).

Before drilling each pilot hole, double-check the anchor locations, this time using a nail to mark the precise center of each pilot hole. The holes should be centered side-to-side on the tree trunk, pointing toward the trunk's internal center. They should also be perpendicular to the length of the treehouse beam and perfectly level with each other. Drill each pilot hole as directed, using a heavy-duty ½" drill bit. It is critical that the hole is level, so monitor the position of the drill bit throughout the operation.

Use a level board as a visual reference to determine the best height and location for your tree anchors.

Use the drill bit to clear the hole of debris. Carefully hand-thread the anchor into the hole, checking for level with a torpedo level as you go. When it becomes too hard to thread by hand, use a large pipe wrench to drive the anchor the rest of the way, working until the collar is tightly compressed against the wood and you can't budge the wrench any further. You might want to use a steel pipe slipped over the wrench handle for added leverage. Check again with the long board and level to make sure the anchors will be level with each other, then install the other anchor.

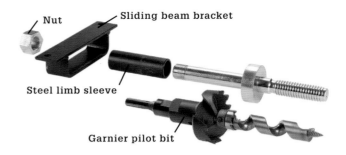

The GL anchor and its specially designed piloting bit. The middle collar section on the anchor compresses into the tree to help prevent rot and disease.

Drill the pilot hole with a heavy-duty ½" drill (available at any rental center). Brace yourself and pay attention to avoid injury with this powerful tool.

Level the anchor carefully as it begins to bite into the tree. A big pipe wrench (and maybe a cheater bar) is the key to getting the anchor tight (below).

Nail three 2 × 10s together to create the built-up rear beam. Stagger the nails between the upper and lower portions of the beam.

With the beam in position, add a nut to the end of each anchor (using a washer, if applicable) to trap the bracket on the anchor.

BUILDING & INSTALLING THE REAR BEAM

Cut three 2 × 10s to length about 24" longer than the outside dimension of the platform frame, so it will overhang the platform about 12" on each end. Crown the boards so any curvature along their length is facing up (convex side of curve is at the top of the beam). Sandwich the boards with their ends aligned and fasten them together with a 20d galvanized nail driven every 32" and two nails at each end.

The beam simply sits on top of the anchors and is secured to each anchor with a sliding or fixed bracket, as applicable. The brackets are a safety backup to keep the beam on top of the anchors during tree movement. Those used here are the sliding-type bracket available from the GL supplier.

Mark the positions of the brackets on the underside of the beam, and install the brackets with lag screws, as directed. Set the beam onto the anchors, slipping the brackets over the ends of the anchors, then add a nut (with a washer, if applicable) to secure the beam.

POURING THE POST FOOTINGS

With the rear beam in place, you can measure from it to create an accurate layout for the two concrete post footings. Transfer the beam's location to the ground, using a plumb bob, and mark the ground with stakes or a string line. Measure straight out from the beam, and mark the centerpoint of each post with a stake. Here, the posts are centered 91¾" from the rear face of the rear beam and are spaced about 10 feet apart. (The front roof posts will bear on the front beam for additional support.)

At each post location, dig a hole for an 8"-diameter concrete tube form, digging below the frost line for your area (check with your local building department for the recommended footing depth), plus 3". Add a 3" layer of gravel and tamp it down. Cut a cardboard tube form to length so it extends 2" above the ground. Set the form in the hole and secure it all around with tamped soil, making sure the form is plumb.

Fill the form with concrete and smooth it off level with the top of the form. Set a ⅝"-diameter J-bolt into the concrete so it extends ¾" to 1" above the concrete (or as directed by the post base manufacturer). Let the concrete cure as directed.

Embed an anchor bolt into the wet concrete of each footing. The bolt should be centered on the footing.

Build the front beam with two 2 × 12 boards, staggering 10d nails with 16" spacing. Shape the ends with decorative cuts, if desired.

Level across from the top of the rear beam to mark the top cutoff lines on the posts.

CONSTRUCT THE FRONT BEAM

The front beam is made with two 2 × 12s nailed together, much like the rear beam. It will sit in notches cut into the top, inside faces of the posts. Cut the two pieces to length to match the rear beam. Crown the boards (convex curve points up), and nail them together with 10d galvanized nails spaced 16" apart, plus two nails on each end. If desired, you can make decorative cuts at the ends of the assembled beam.

PREPARING THE POSTS

Install a post base with a standoff plate on top of each footing, using a washer and nut secured to the anchor bolt. Set an 8-foot.-long 6 × 6 post onto each base, plumb the post in both directions, and secure it in place with 2 × 4 cross bracing. You can tack the post to the base with one nail to keep it from slipping.

With both posts plumbed and braced, level over from the rear beam with a long, straight board. Mark each post with a level line that is precisely level with the top of the beam. This line represents the top of the post, where you will cut the post to its final length.

Remove the posts from their bases. Measure the depth (top-to-bottom dimension) and thickness of the front beam. Using these dimensions, mark a notch onto the rear and side faces of each post.

Use a square to extend the cutting lines across the post faces for the top end cutoff and notches.

The top of the notch is the top cutoff line you made in the last step. Cut each post at the top cutoff line, using a circular saw to cut along all four sides, then finish the cut through the center with a handsaw or reciprocating saw with a long wood blade. Cut out the notches using the same technique.

INSTALLING THE POSTS & FRONT BEAM

Set the posts back in their bases and brace them plumb, as before. Set the front beam onto the notches of the posts (with the crown of the beam pointing up) so the beam overhangs the posts equally on both ends. Clamp the beam to the posts or tack it in place with nails. Confirm that the posts are plumb (you can adjust the base positions a bit, if needed), then anchor the posts to the bases with the manufacturer's specified fasteners (for the bases shown, you can use galvanized nails or machine bolts, but not both).

Anchor each beam to its post with two ⅜" carriage bolts with washers. Drill a counterbore for the washers and nuts on the rear face of the beam. When all the nuts are tightened, fill the counterbores with caulk to prevent water intrusion and forestall rot.

Tack a couple of 2 × 4s across the tops of the beams to help brace the front beam and posts. Leave the posts' cross bracing (installed earlier) in place until the treehouse platform is completed.

Fasten the posts to their bases. Make sure the base is tightened down to the anchor bolt with the provided nut.

Beam side

Fasten the front beam to the posts with pairs of carriage bolts inserted through the posts and secured on the beam side with washers and nuts.

ADDING THE KNEE BRACES

The two knee braces provide lateral support for the posts and add a traditional timber-frame look to the treehouse structure. They're cut from a 10-foot 6 × 6 and meet the posts and front beam at a 45° angle. *Note: All bracing for your project should be designed to suit your specific site conditions and house design.*

Cut a 10-foot 6 × 6 in half, then miter one end of each piece at 45°. Mark the front face of each post about 36" down from the top of the front beam. Position each brace against the post and beam, with the long point of its mitered end aligned with the mark and its rear face against the front of the beam. Trace along the top and bottom of the beam onto the brace;

these cuts represent the top cut and bottom of the notch for the beam.

On the inside portion of each brace, lay out the notch to match the thickness of the front beam. Cut the top end of the braces at 45°, then cut the notches with a circular saw and handsaw or reciprocating saw, as before.

Set each brace in position so its bottom end is on the original mark and its side faces are flush with the front and rear post faces. The top cut should be flush with the top of the beam. Clamp both ends of the brace in place. Drill counterbored pilot holes, and fasten the brace to the beam with two ⅜" carriage bolts and to the post with two ⅜" × 7 lag screws with washers.

Trace along the front beam to mark the top cuts and notches for the knee braces. When installed, the faces of the posts and braces are aligned.

Anchor the knee braces to the posts with lag screws driven straight through the inside faces of the braces, roughly centered on the joint.

Use a scrap of 6 × 6 post as a spacer when marking the joist layout and installing the joists. The roof posts should fit snugly between the joist pairs.

Metal framing connectors create a strong connection between the treehouse platform and the beams and are important for resisting wind uplift.

FRAMING THE PLATFORM

Cut two 2 × 8 rim joists to run the full length of the platform, then cut 11 2 × 8 joists equal to the full width (front to back) of the platform, minus 3". Mark the joist layout onto the rim joists, using a scrap piece of 6 × 6 post to set the spaces for the eight roof posts. The four corner posts are set 1½" in from the end of each rim joist, and the two remaining posts on each side are spaced evenly in between. Gang the rim joists together to mark the layout, to ensure that all joists and posts are properly aligned.

Assemble the platform frame on top of the beams. Start by nailing the rear rim joist to all of the joists,

using three 16d nails for each. Then, move to the front of the frame and nail the front rim joist onto the ends of the joists. When the frame is assembled, center it side-to-side over both beams, and measure diagonally between opposing corners to check for square: When the measurements are equal the frame is square. Tack the frame to the beam with several nails to hold it in place, then reinforce the connection with metal framing connectors (consult a building professional or your local building department for recommendations on the best connectors for your project).

Follow chalk lines to set the initial rows of decking (since you can't start at the edge of the platform). A few extra chalk lines can help you stay on track during the installation.

DECKING THE PLATFORM

The platform frame is decked with 2 × 6 or 5/4 × 6 boards to create the treehouse floor. Thinner 5/4 × 6 decking is suitable for up to 24" of joist spacing if the wood is pine or hemlock; for cedar and redwood, 2 × 6 decking is recommended. At this stage, most of the decking is installed to facilitate working from the platform, but a few boards are left off at each side to provide access for installing the roof posts.

Use a scrap piece of your decking material to mark layout lines on the joists. This is to ensure that you won't reach the edge of the platform and discover that the last board is just a sliver. The decking should run perpendicular to the interior joists (parallel to the rim joists) and stop flush with the outside faces of the two outside joists.

Step off each row of decking, leaving a ¼" gap between rows for drainage and easy cleaning, working from the front edge of the platform to the rear. If the last board is less than half a width, plan to rip down the boards of the starting row (at the front) so the starting and end rows are roughly equal in width. Once you're satisfied with the layout, snap chalk lines to guide the installation.

Following your layout, install the decking with deck screws sized for the decking material. Drill pilot holes, and drive two screws at each joist connection. Remember not to install the last few rows of decking at the front and rear of the platform.

INSTALLING THE ROOF POSTS

The 6 × 6 roof posts extend from the bottom of the platform frame to the tops of the rafters. They support the entire roof structure as well as the treehouse railing. Cut the top ends of each 8-foot 6 × 6 post at a 33.7° angle; this follows the 8-in-12 slope of the roof.

Then, measuring from the long point of the beveled end, cut the post to length with a square cut, based on the desired height of the roof. For the project shown, the roof posts are about 89" long from the square bottom end to the long point of the top end.

Set each corner post into its place between the closely spaced pairs of platform joists. Clamp it between the joists so it stands perfectly plumb and its bottom end is flush with the bottom of the joists, resting on the beam below. Drill pilot holes, and fasten the post to both neighboring joists with four ⅜" carriage bolts. You don't have to counterbore for these bolts, but the bolt heads should be on the outsides of the outer joists.

Run a taut string line between the two corner posts on each side of the platform, parallel to the beams. Install the two remaining posts on each side in the same manner, using the string line to make sure all four posts are aligned.

Complete the platform decking to fill in the openings left for the post installation. Notch the deck boards as needed to fit around the posts. The decking should be flush with the outsides of the platform frame.

Anchor the bottom ends of the roof posts with carriage bolts, sandwiching the posts between the joists at either side.

Use a string line to ensure the posts are on the same plane across each side of the treehouse.

19

Cut the ends of the pattern rafters at 33.7° and test-fit them on a pair of roof posts, using a piece of 2 × 8 scrap to serve as the ridge beam.

CUTTING THE RAFTERS

The roof is framed much like a standard gable roof, but here the rafters are easier to cut because they have no bird's mouth cuts. Instead of sitting atop the walls, the rafters here simply fasten to the sides of the roof posts. Cut two 2 × 6 pattern rafters with an 8-in-12 slope (33.7°), following the techniques described on pages 118 to 119. Use a scrap of 2 × 8 to represent the ridge beam. The tops of the rafters should be flush with the top ends of the roof posts and extend about 8" (measured horizontally) beyond the outsides of the posts.

Use the pattern rafters to mark and cut the remaining 14 rafters, for a total of 16. Cut the 2 × 8 ridge beam to length so it overhangs the outer roof posts by about 4½", or as desired.

FRAMING THE ROOF

Mark the rafter layout onto the ridge beam by clamping the ridge across the roof posts on one side of the treehouse so the ridge is flush with the tops of the posts and overhangs the outer posts equally on both ends (photo 20). Trace along both side faces of each post; these lines represent the inside faces of the rafters. Use a square to transfer the marks to the other face of the ridge.

Install the four outermost rafters and ridge beam, using 16d galvanized nails. Drive four nails through each rafter and into the roof post, and use two nails to fasten the rafter to the ridge. Next, install the pairs of rafters on the outside faces of the two sets of interior posts. At this point, only one side of each post has a rafter on it.

Cut the two 2 × 6 interior rafter ties to span between the rafter pairs so their bottom edges are about 80" above the platform deck. Make sure the ties are level, and fasten them to the inside faces of the rafters with 2½" screws at each end.

To create the truss detail at each gable end of the roof frame, cut a 2 × 6 rafter tie to span between the rafters so their bottom edges are about 76" above the platform deck. Fasten these to the inside faces of the outermost rafters. Next, cut a 2 × 6 strut to fit between the top of the rafter tie (gable ends only) and the tops of the rafters, cutting the top end of the strut to a point. Then, notch the strut's top end to fit snugly around the ridge beam. Nail the strut to the top edge of the rafter tie and to the rafters and ridge beam.

Install the remaining rafters to complete the roof frame.

20

Mark the ridge beam for rafters, using the roof posts. Make an "X" to the outside of each post marking to show where the rafter goes.

21

Interior rafter ties span across the rafters on the interior roof posts. Their ends are cut to match the roof slope.

INSTALLING THE ROOF DECK & ROOFING

The decking material for the roof is ⅝" or ¾" T&G roof sheathing rated for a 40" rafter span. Since the underside and edges of the sheathing will remain exposed, it's best to use "Exterior" sheathing (as opposed to "Exposure 1" or "Exposure 2"). As an optional addition, you can install ⅜" cedar plywood on the underside of the sheathing, to create a decorative "ceiling" finish.

Install the roof decking following the techniques described on page 122, overhanging the outermost rafters by about 3" at the gable ends of the roof. If desired, cover the underside of the roof deck with exterior cedar plywood (or other outdoor material), using construction adhesive and short trim screws or brads.

Complete the roof with building paper and asphalt (composition) shingle roofing, following the techniques described on pages 122 through 124. If you chose to cover the underside of the deck with decorative plywood, be sure the roofing nails are short enough that they won't come through the plywood.

The gable-end rafter ties are combined with a strut to create a truss detail. The strut is notched to fit around the ridge beam (inset).

Tongue-and-groove roof decking is required for the relatively wide spans of the rafters. Follow the manufacturer's specifications for gapping between panels.

A decorative layer of cedar plywood conceals roofing nails and creates a finished ceiling. Notch the panels as needed to fit around the roof framing.

Composition shingles make for an inexpensive, long-lasting roof. Consider the shingle color carefully, as you'll probably be looking at it most of the year.

BUILDING THE RAILING

The railing has horizontal 2 × 4 rails that support 2 × 2 balusters, much like you find with many deck designs. The top of the railing gets a 2 × 6 cap, which makes a nice surface to lean against to enjoy a view or to set down drinks. You can modify the railing design as desired, but make sure yours meets the minimum standards for safety: Most importantly, the railing must be at least 36" tall, from the deck surface to the top of the railing, and the balusters must be spaced just under 4" apart (if a 4"-diameter ball can fit between the balusters, they're too far apart); see page 93 for more railing design and safety information.

To install the 2 × 4 rails, make two marks on each corner roof post, 7½" and 34½" up from the treehouse floor. Snap chalk lines across all of the roof posts at these marks; the lines represent the top edges of the 2 × 4 rails.

Cut the 2 × 4 rails to span across the roof posts, using single pieces for each run, if possible. You can wrap around the outsides of the posts with mitered or butted joints. Fasten through the rails and into the posts with 3" deck screws. *Note: If you want to create built-in*

stops on the latch side of the gate opening, extend the rails about 1½" into the opening, as shown on page 182).

Mark the baluster layout onto the inside faces of the rails. Create a layout for each space between neighboring posts, working from the center so that the gaps between balusters is the same at both ends of the space.

Cut the 2 × 2 balusters to length so they extend from the top of the top rail to the bottom edge of the bottom rail, mitering the bottom ends, if desired. Position each baluster so it's flush with the top of the top rail, check it for plumb, and fasten it with 2½" deck screws.

To install the 2 × 6 railing caps, rough-cut each piece a little longer than you need. Set the board in place on top of the top rail, on the outside of the roof posts, and mark the positions of the posts onto the cap. Notch the cap at the marks, setting the notch depth so that the cap will overhang the outsides of the rails by 1½". Test-fit the cap, then mark the ends for final cuts. It looks best if you miter the caps at the corner joints. Fasten the caps to the rails and the balusters (as needed) with 3" deck screws.

Install the rails with their top edges on the chalk lines. The 3" gap below the bottom rail makes it easy to sweep off the treehouse deck.

Use a baluster and level to mark the sides of each baluster location, and use a 2 × 4 block cut to length at 3⅞" to set the gaps between balusters.

Notch the caps to fit around the posts (inset), leaving about a 1½" overhang on the outside of the railing and a 1" overhang on the inside.

29

Self-closing hinges keep the gate closed when it's not in use—a handy safety feature for anyone using the treehouse.

CONSTRUCT THE GATE

The gate shown here is built just like the railing and is hung with self-closing hinges, with the gate swinging in for safety. Another important safety (and longevity) feature is a stop that supports the gate when it's closed and prevents it from being pushed through the wrong way. Notches cut into the rails and caps of the railing and gate create strong, built-in stops that require no hardware.

Build the gate with the same materials and baluster spacing used for the treehouse railing, making it a little narrower than the gate opening to allow for hinge and swing clearance. Reinforce the gate with a turnbuckle and rods (running from the top hinge corner to the bottom latch corner) or a wood or metal cross brace (running from the top latch corner to the bottom hinge corner). Hang the gate with heavy-duty self-closing hinges mounted to the roof post.

30

Swing direction →

Mating notches in the caps and rails of the gate and treehouse railing create safety stops that also prevent undue wear and tear on the gate.

PROVIDING ACCESS & ACCESSORIES

Given its versatile, "all-ages" design, this treehouse should have a relatively pedestrian means of access, such as sturdy ladder steps or even a full-fledged staircase. If you won't use the house during the cold months of the year, you might prefer to use ladder steps that you can remove so the house is inaccessible in the off-season.

As for accessories, you can hang all manner of climbing and play things from the front beam and platform joists—swings, trapeze, knotted climbing rope, rings, you name it. The posts are ideal for stringing up a hammock, either in the treehouse or down below between the platform posts. You could even hang a little two-seater porch swing from the rafter ties.

Access to this treehouse happens to be at the front, but it could also be at either end or even the back, if you'd prefer a cleaner look at the front.

Strategically placed accessories, such as swings and climbing ropes, turn the treehouse into the best kind of backyard play structure.

Gable House with Entry Deck

A treehouse that feels like a home. Solid walls, sturdy windows and doors, and some simple decorative touches add up to a cozy retreat where kids can really let their imaginations run wild.

This nicely proportioned house is a great example of what you can do with one good, stout tree. And the design is simpler than it looks. It starts with a square platform that's framed around the trunk and supported by knee braces at the corners. Apart from the cutout for the door and entry deck, the house is just a box with a gable roof, much like the houses you find in kids' drawings. This classic look is no coincidence—with its traditional lines and fully enclosed interior, the treehouse has an especially homey feel, a theme that's enhanced by the Dutch door and playhouse-size entry deck. The interior layout also lends itself to built-in accessories, like shelves and tables.

A single-tree house of this size requires a large, mature tree. The specimen must be healthy, of course,

and should measure at least 5 feet in circumference at its base. Because the tree alone will bear the burden of the house and its occupants, it's a good idea to have it inspected by an arborist before making any serious construction plans. Think about where you'd like to place the house, so you can give special attention to the installation areas.

Note: The instructions here provide a detailed overview of building the house as shown, for this particular site. They can serve as a general guide to help you design and build a similar house of your own. However, all of the construction specifications for your project must be geared for your specific house design, the intended use of the house, the tree, and the building site, as well as any applicable local building codes and zoning restrictions.

Self-closing hinges keep the gate shut when it's not in use—a handy safety feature for anyone using the treehouse.

Gable House with Entry Deck

GABLE HOUSE EXPLODED VIEW

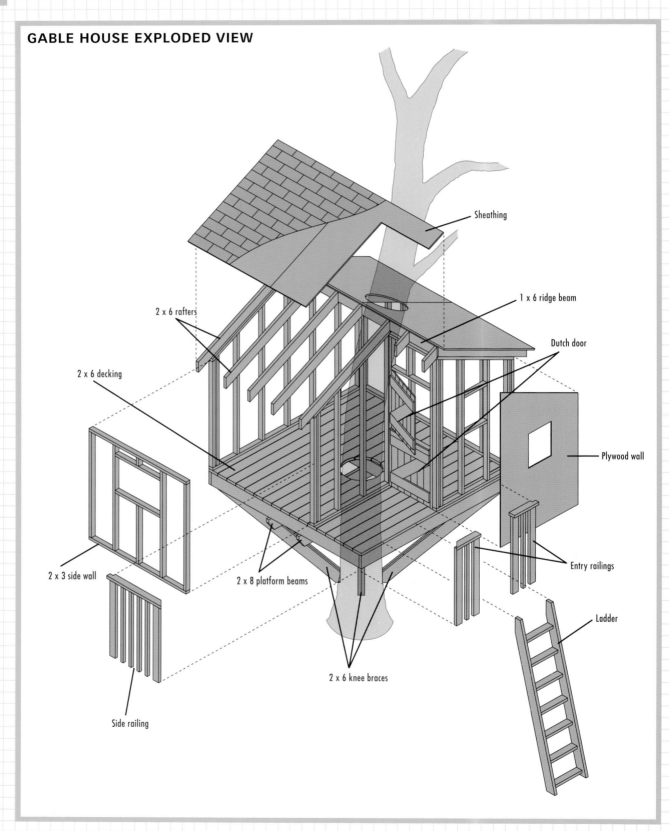

Sheathing

1 x 6 ridge beam

2 x 6 rafters

Dutch door

2 x 6 decking

Plywood wall

2 x 3 side wall

Entry railings

2 x 8 platform beams

Ladder

2 x 6 knee braces

Side railing

PLATFORM FRAMING

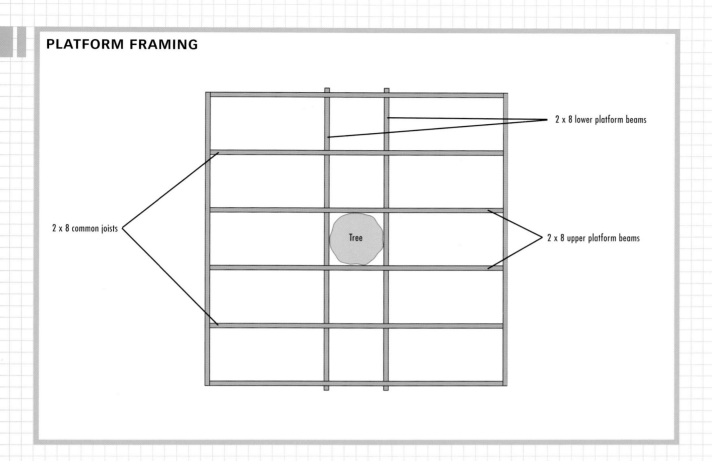

2 x 8 lower platform beams

2 x 8 common joists

Tree

2 x 8 upper platform beams

FRONT ELEVATION

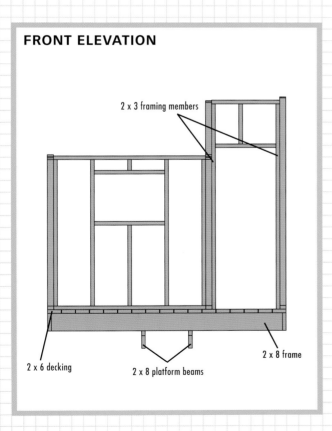

2 x 3 framing members

2 x 6 decking

2 x 8 platform beams

2 x 8 frame

SIDE ELEVATION LEFT

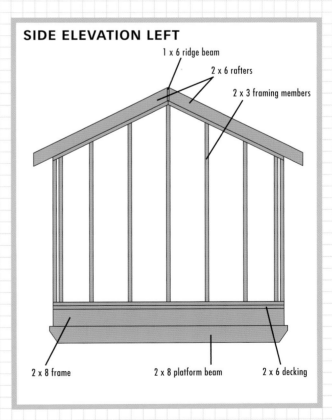

1 x 6 ridge beam

2 x 6 rafters

2 x 3 framing members

2 x 8 frame

2 x 8 platform beam

2 x 6 decking

FLOOR PLAN

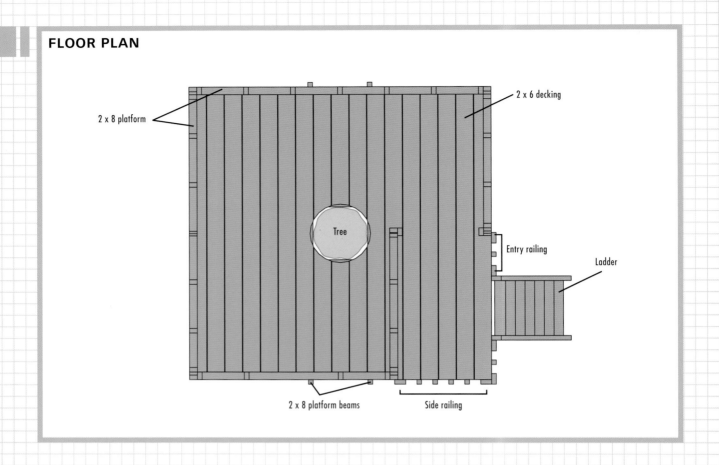

2 x 8 platform

2 x 6 decking

Tree

Entry railing

Ladder

2 x 8 platform beams

Side railing

BACK ELEVATION

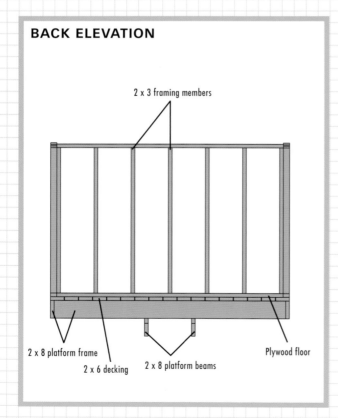

2 x 3 framing members

2 x 8 platform frame

2 x 6 decking

2 x 8 platform beams

Plywood floor

SIDE ELEVATION RIGHT

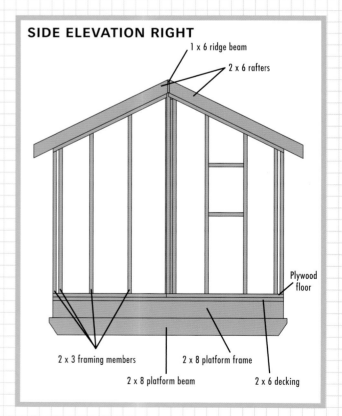

1 x 6 ridge beam

2 x 6 rafters

Plywood floor

2 x 3 framing members

2 x 8 platform frame

2 x 8 platform beam

2 x 6 decking

INSTALLING THE PLATFORM BEAMS

The treehouse platform has four 2 × 8 beams, all of which are anchored to the tree with a single ¾" lag screw and washers. Cut the lower pair of beams to the full width of the platform. If desired, angle-cut the bottom corners of the beams for decorative embellishment. Mark the tree at the desired height of the finished platform minus 8¾" (the combined depth of the platform frame and decking); this represents the top edges of the lower beams.

Drill clearance holes in the beams and pilot holes in the tree, and anchor the beams to the tree following the techniques described for fixed anchors, on page 61. The lag screws should be centered along the length of the beam and point towards the center of the tree trunk. Make sure the second beam is perfectly level with the first before installing it.

Cut the two upper beams to the full length of the platform minus 3". These beams are integrated into the platform frame and are the same length as the common joists. Install the upper beams perpendicular to the lower beams, with their bottom edges resting on the lower beams.

INSTALLING THE JOISTS & KNEE BRACES

In the project as shown, the platform frame was assembled before the knee braces were installed.

Initially, 2 × 6 knee braces were anchored to the tree with special brackets (see page 190), then an additional 2 × 6 was sistered to each brace for added rigidity. For your own project, you might prefer to install the knee braces after only the perimeter joists are installed. It's also an option to use 4 × 6s for the knee braces; however, this requires a specially sized bracket that may need to be custom-fabricated. *Note: Don't use the platform for support until the knee braces are installed.*

Cut the two 2 × 8 rim joists to match the length of the lower beams, and cut the four 2 × 8 common joists to the same length as the upper beams (your project may call for more joists, depending on the size of the platform and the decking material). Set the common joists on edge atop the lower beams, and fasten one of the rim joists to each common joist with three 16d nails or 3½" deck screws. Install the other rim joist on the other ends of the commons.

Square up the frame using a framing square (you can't measure the diagonals, because the tree is in the way), and toenail the frame to the lower beams with 16d nails. Level the platform in both directions, then secure it in position with a few temporary posts extending to the ground.

Anchor the lower beams to the center of the tree. Remember that the lag screws should be just below center (top-to-bottom) on the beams.

Install the upper beams, checking all of the beams for level as you go. If necessary, use wood shims to make a beam stand plumb against the tree (inset).

Cut the knee braces so they fit between the inside of each corner of the platform frame and extend down to the tree at a 45° angle. Cut the top ends of the braces at 45°, and cut the bottom ends to fit the anchor brackets. Use the knee braces to mark the precise locations of the anchor brackets, and install the brackets as directed by the manufacturer. The brackets used here are installed with a single lag screw to the tree (don't use two fasteners close together, which promotes tree rot) and a single lag screw into the end of the knee brace.

Install the braces, toenailing the top ends to the platform frame, then reinforcing each joint with a framing connector. Add a second knee brace, if applicable, sistering the two with 10d nails or 3" deck screws.

DECKING THE PLATFORM

Install the 2 × 6 (or 5/4 × 6) decking so it runs perpendicular to the common joists and is flush with outside of the framing on all sides. Fasten deck boards to each joist with pairs of 3" deck screws. Be sure to leave a 2" gap between the decking and the tree to allow for growth.

Because the house's interior will be enclosed, you don't have to leave gaps between the boards for drainage, if you prefer not to. However, you might want to gap them a bit for expansion, and larger gaps make for easier cleaning. If you prefer a continuous floor surface, you can also save some money by using plywood instead of 2 × 6s.

Secure the knee braces to the tree with anchor brackets (inset) and to the platform frame with toenailed screws or nails and framing connectors.

Custom fit the decking boards around the tree by butting each piece up to the tree and using a compass set at 2" to transfer the tree's contours to the board.

Fasten the rim joists to the common joists with nails or screws. Here, the interior common joists are centered between the outer commons and the upper beams.

The left gable wall spans the width of the house and is centered on the roof peak. The extra stud at each end is for installing interior finishes.

BUILDING THE WALLS

The walls of this house are framed with 2 × 3 lumber and are small enough that they can be framed and sided on the ground, then hoisted up onto the platform for installation. The left and right sides of the house have gable walls that create the roof slope. The left gable is one assembly, while the right gable is made up of two sections separated by a short section of the front wall, creating a jog that becomes the door wall. The single rear wall and two front walls are standard rectangular walls.

Start the framing with the left gable wall, following the techniques described on pages 83 and 84. The roof shown here has a slope of 6-in-12, so the top ends of the studs are cut at 26.6°. Frame the two right gable wall sections so that each one matches one half of the left wall. The rear section gets a rough opening for a custom-made window at any size or height you like.

Frame the rear wall to the same height as the sides of the left gable wall; make this a butt wall (see page 83) that will fit inside the two adjacent gable walls. Determine the size of the door wall based on the desired width of the door, adding several inches at either side of the door. The door wall section will act as a butt wall at the right side of the house and as a through wall where it meets the front half of the left gable wall. Frame the other front wall section to include a salvaged or homemade window, if desired.

When all the walls are framed, tip them up for a quick test assembly. Check the outside dimensions of the assembly, and make sure the walls are square and are aligned properly for the roof planes. This is also the time to plan the siding installation and figure out

where the siding should overhang the framing to cover the end of the mating wall, as applicable.

Install the siding according to your plan. The material used here is ⅜" cedar plywood siding; see page 87 for basic installation steps.

INSTALLING THE WALLS

Snap chalk lines on the treehouse deck to guide the installation. Raise and install the walls following the basic process discussed on page 92. For this project, the corner trim isn't added until the end of the house construction.

Use ropes and a pulley, a block and tackle, or any other mechanical aids to hoist the walls up to the platform.

Fasten the walls together at the corners with deck screws, following the same plan you used for the dry assembly on the ground.

Installing the ridge beam first makes it easy to mark and test-fit the pattern rafters.

The rafters overhang the front and rear walls by about 8" (measured horizontally) to create the traditional eaves.

FRAMING THE ROOF

This house's roof has an eave overhang along the gabled sides as well as the bottom edges at the front and rear. To create the gable extensions, simply cut the 1 × 6 ridge beam so it overhangs the left and right sides of the house by about 6", or as desired. Mark the rafter layout on the ridge, then tack the ridge in place with a few nails.

Cut two 2 × 6 pattern rafters, following the steps described on pages 118 to 119. These are for the common (full-size) rafters; later, you will make custom-sized rafters for the gables and the roof overhang above the door. Use the patterns to mark and cut the remaining seven common rafters. The front section of the roof gets three commons, and the rear section gets six commons. Install the common rafters.

Cut the custom rafters along the gables so they sit on top of the wall plates and their top edges are level with the tops of the common rafters. These rafters don't get bird's mouth cuts, so their bottom edges on the eave ends are a little higher than those of the common rafters. Install the gable rafters.

Finally, cut and install the three short rafters along the door wall. These should extend roughly the same distance as the eave ends of the common rafters. Install the short rafters by toenailing them to the ridge beam.

The custom gable rafters are installed so their outside faces are flush with the outside of the wall siding.

COMPLETING THE ROOF

The treehouse can have any roofing material you like. Here, the roofing is asphalt (composition) shingles laid over ½" plywood sheathing. Because the edges and some of the underside of the sheathing will remain exposed, it's best to use "Exterior" sheathing (as opposed to "Exposure 1" or "Exposure 2"), which is designed for permanent exposure. Sheathe and shingle the roof following the techniques on pages 122 through 124.

ADDING THE WINDOWS

The treehouse as shown has two windows. One is an octagonal window bought at an architectural salvage shop, a great place to find one-of-a-kind windows and other curiosities for a treehouse. You can also find used windows at building materials recyclers (including Habitat for Humanity outlets) and antique shops. The octagonal window shown here came

Preassembling a homemade window can save you some trips to and from the treehouse, but it requires careful measuring of the window opening.

Salvaged windows with exterior trim are a breeze to install. Others might call for some creative carpentry, but they're well worth the effort.

with exterior trim ("brick molding") attached. It was installed by nailing through the molding and into the wall siding and framing with galvanized casing nails. A continuous bead of exterior caulk applied along the perimeter of the molding prevents leaks.

The other window is totally handmade from 1× and 2× lumber, some molding, and polycarbonate sheeting for the "glass." The steps on pages 106 through 112 walk you through the process of building your own window to any size you need. You can create the window piece-by-piece right in the rough opening of the wall, or you can use the same basic process and assemble the parts on the ground, then install the completed window in the opening.

To install a pre-assembled window, center the window frame inside the rough opening of the wall, with the window sill resting on the 2 × 3 rough sill and the horns of the sill tight against the outside of the siding. Use tapered cedar shims, if necessary, to snug the side and top jambs to the rough opening. Fasten through the jambs and sill and into the framing with galvanized finish nails. Another option is to pre-install the trim on the window unit, allowing you to fasten the window through the front of the trim and into the siding and framing.

BUILDING THE DUTCH DOOR

The Dutch door adds some fun to the house design and even some practicality: closing the bottom half of the door keeps little ones safely corralled inside the house without having to shut off the opening entirely. Of course, a standard door would work just fine for the house, too. Instructions for building both door types are given on page 115.

The Dutch door shown here essentially is two short versions on the standard Z-brace door. Construct the two doors to fit the rough opening frame, leaving about ⅞" between the doors for a 1 × 4 shelf at the top of the bottom door, plus a ⅛" gap for clearance. Hang the doors so they swing out toward the front gable wall. Install 1 × 4 trim along the outside edges of the jambs, and add a latch to the lower door. Align the doors and install a slide bolt or barrel bolt (one that locks in the retracted position) onto the upper door so the barrel extends straight down into a hole (with a metal plate, if desired) in the lower door, to latch the doors together.

INSTALL THE RAILING & LADDER

For this particular project, the railing and ladder were left off until now to facilitate construction, but you could add either whenever it's convenient.

To build the railing, cut six 2 × 4 posts to length at 43¼" (or longer, if you prefer to make the railing higher than the code minimum of 36" above the platform decking). Install one post at each end of the railing, overlapping the house wall by 1½" or so, and install two posts at the outside corner of the platform, forming an "L" with one post overlapping the edge of the other. Install the last two posts at the outsides of the ladder opening. Anchor each post to the platform joist with two 3" lag screws and washers driven through pilot holes. Also fasten the end posts to the treehouse walls. The posts should be perfectly plumb, with their bottom ends flush with the bottom edges of the joists.

Cut pieces of 2 × 4 railing cap to span over the tops of the neighboring posts (except within the ladder opening). Round the corners of the caps and sand the edges to remove sharpness and prevent splintering. Fasten the caps to the posts with 3½" deck screws so the inside edges of the caps overhang the insides of the posts by 1½".

Cut 2 × 2 support cleats to run along the inside faces of the posts, and install them up against the cap using 2½" screws driven into the posts and cap. Cut the 2 × 2 balusters to the same length as the posts.

Install the balusters with even spacing so the resulting gaps are no more than 4". Fasten the balusters to the platform joists with pairs of 3" deck screws and to the support cleats with 2½" deck screws.

Access to this house is provided by a flat-rung ladder. Instructions for this are on page 128. Other good options include a double-rung ladder (pages 126 and 127) and conventional outdoor stairs (pages 130 to 133). If you choose to build a ladder, be sure to include a safety rail running across the top of the ladder opening in the treehouse railing.

This sample Dutch door shows the simple construction of tongue-and-groove siding boards joined with 1 × 6 Z-bracing.

This simple railing is made with 2 × 4s and 2 × 2s anchored to the platform framing and the house walls.

FINISHING THE HOUSE

If you used plywood siding on the walls, now is the time to add the 1 × 4 corner trim at the outside corners of the house. Basic techniques for installing trim are covered on pages 90 to 91. The corner trim material should match or complement the exterior trim for the house's windows and door.

Now it's time to add color. This house design looks great with a semi-transparent stain on the plywood siding and dark paint on the trim, door, and roof structure. Painting the siding can work well, too,

but stick with a contrasting color for the trim and roof to add definition to the building and make the trim details "pop." The railing also should be finished to prevent premature weathering and roughening of the wood.

Inside the house, a few thoughtfully placed features can create a fun and functional living space. Finish the walls with paneling and trim, build a custom flip-down bunk or two, or add a flip-up table and a few shelves. See pages 96 through 103 for help with these and other custom projects.

More Treehouse Plans

No two treehouses are exactly alike because no two trees are the same. But that doesn't mean building plans are worthless when it comes to treehouses. In fact, we've decided to wrap up this book by including six fully developed plans for your consideration and inspiration. It's unlikely that you'll be able to use them exactly as they are shown, so we've left out some dimensions and details that you'll need to fill in yourself based on your tree or trees and on your needs and plans. But we think you'll find them to be a good leaping off point for your venture into the trees.

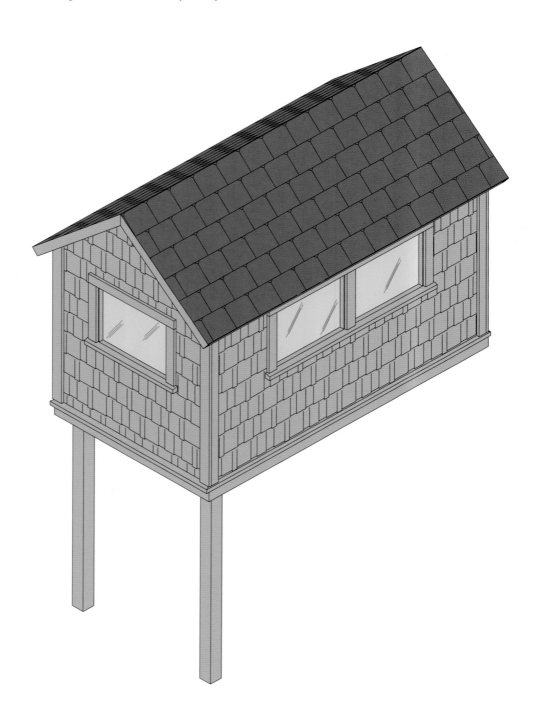

Plan 1: Gable Roof with Auxiliary Posts

EXPLODED ISOMETRIC

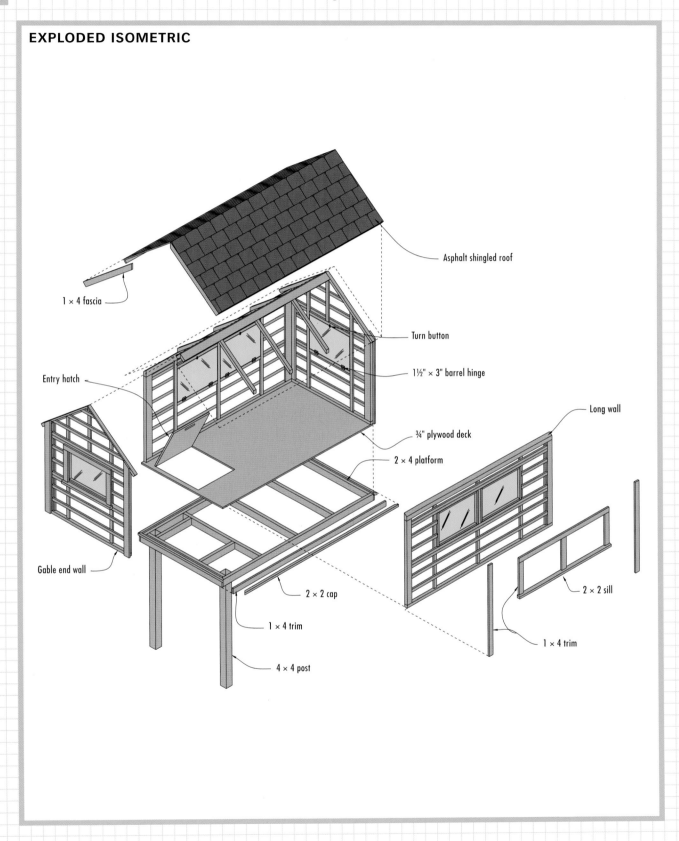

Asphalt shingled roof

1 × 4 fascia

Turn button

1½" × 3" barrel hinge

Entry hatch

¾" plywood deck

2 × 4 platform

Long wall

Gable end wall

2 × 2 cap

2 × 2 sill

1 × 4 trim

1 × 4 trim

4 × 4 post

ELEVATION: GABLE END WALL FRAMING

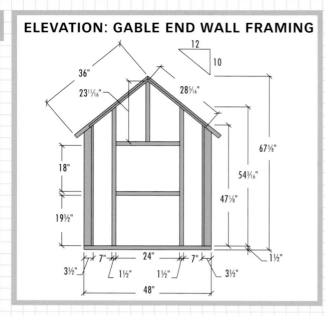

ELEVATION: LONG WALL FRAMING

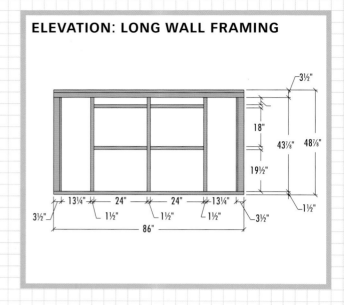

ELEVATION: GABLE END WALL W/SKIP SHEATHING

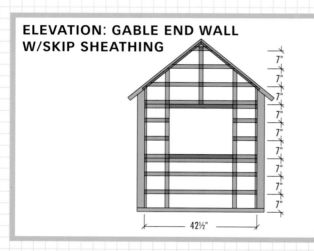

ELEVATION: LONG WALL W/SKIP SHEATHING

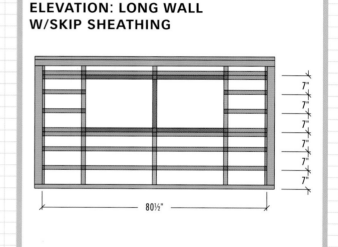

ELEVATION: GABLE END WALL W/TRIM & SHAKES

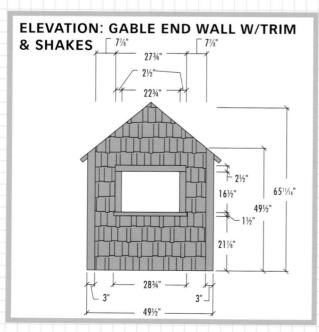

ELEVATION: LONG WALL W/TRIM & SHAKES

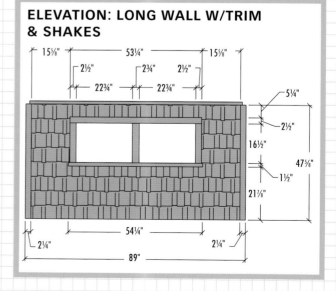

PLAN VIEW: PLATFORM FRAMING

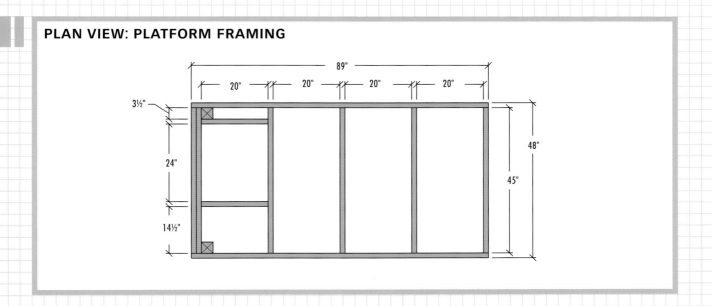

PLAN VIEW: PLYWOOD FLOOR & CUT-OUT

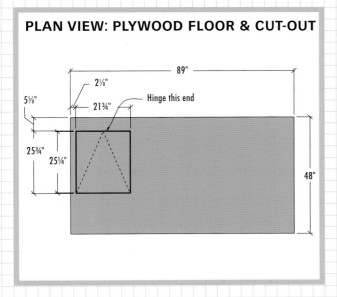

WALL SECTION

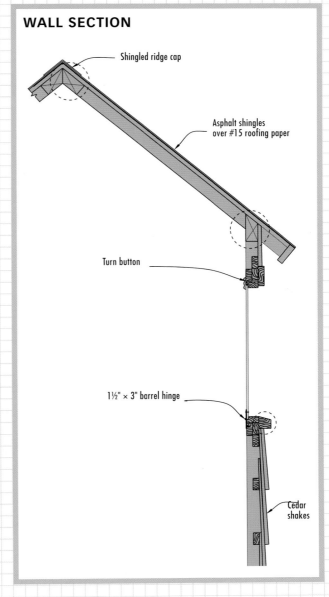

Shingled ridge cap

Asphalt shingles over #15 roofing paper

Turn button

1½" × 3" barrel hinge

Cedar shakes

PLAN VIEW: WALL FRAMING

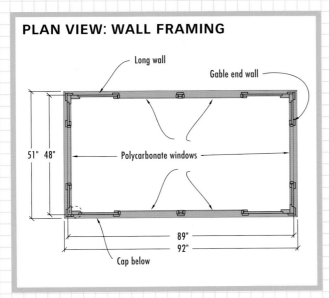

Long wall

Gable end wall

Polycarbonate windows

51" 48"

89"

92"

Cap below

Plan 2: A-Frame with Walkout Deck

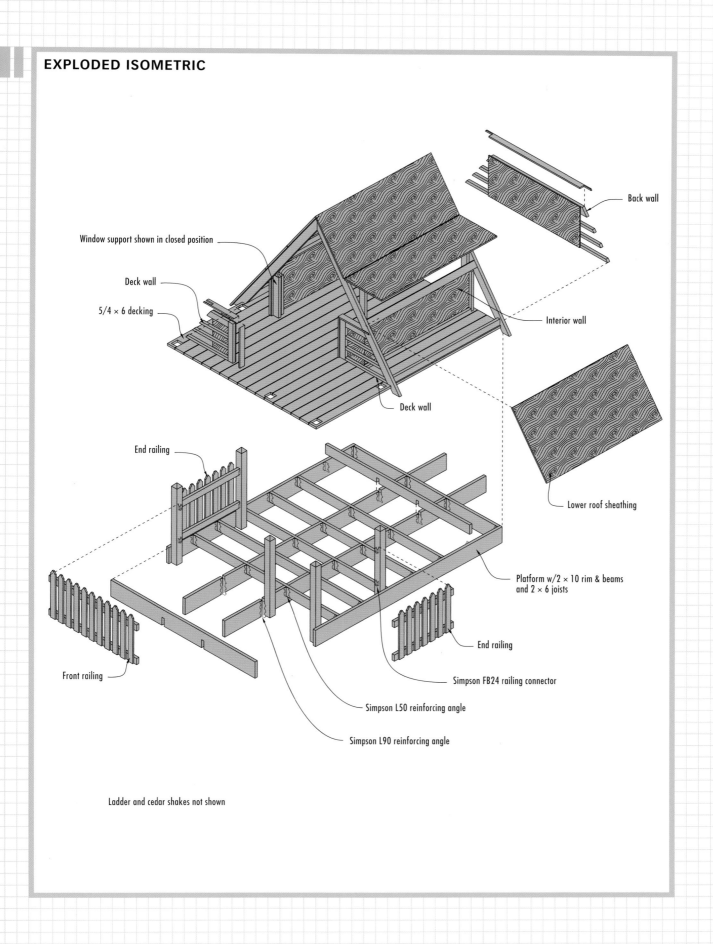

Window support shown in closed position

Deck wall

5/4 × 6 decking

Back wall

Interior wall

Deck wall

Lower roof sheathing

End railing

Platform w/2 × 10 rim & beams
and 2 × 6 joists

End railing

Front railing

Simpson FB24 railing connector

Simpson L50 reinforcing angle

Simpson L90 reinforcing angle

Ladder and cedar shakes not shown

ELEVATION: FRONT WITH STAIRS

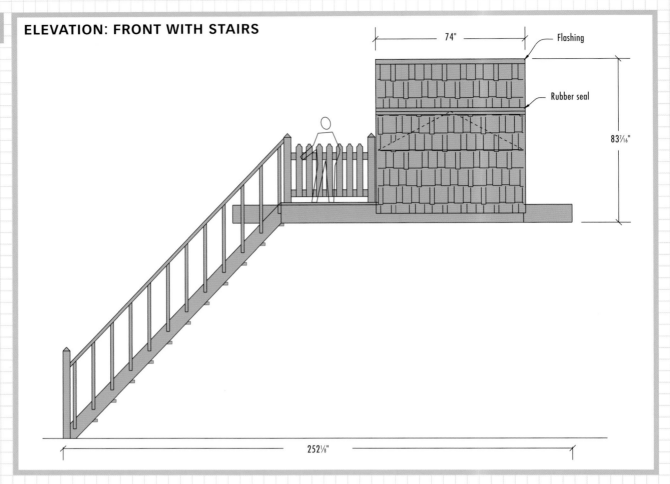

74"

Flashing

Rubber seal

83⁷⁄₁₆"

252⅛"

ELEVATION AT BACK

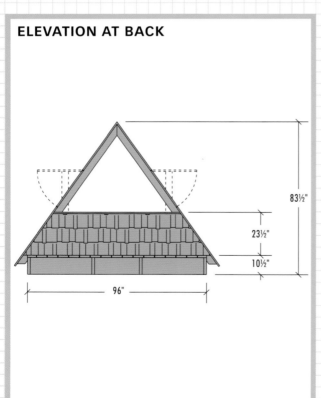

83½"

23½"

10½"

96"

ELEVATION AT DECK (LADDER SHOWN)

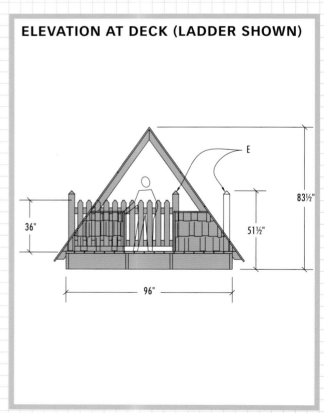

E

83½"

36"

51½"

96"

PLAN VIEW: PLATFORM

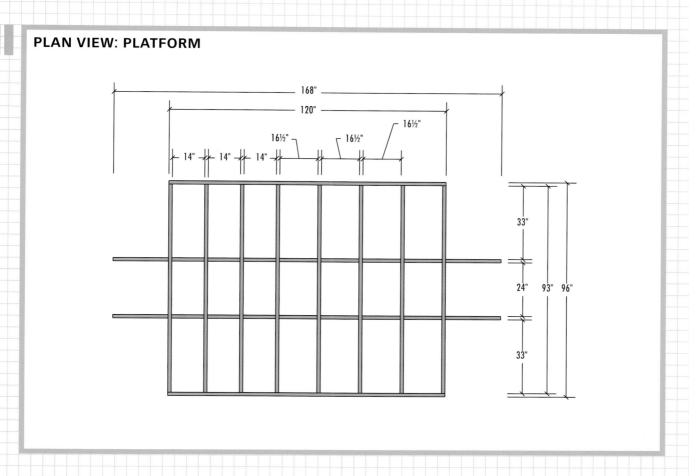

PLAN VIEW: DECK/RAILING/WALLS

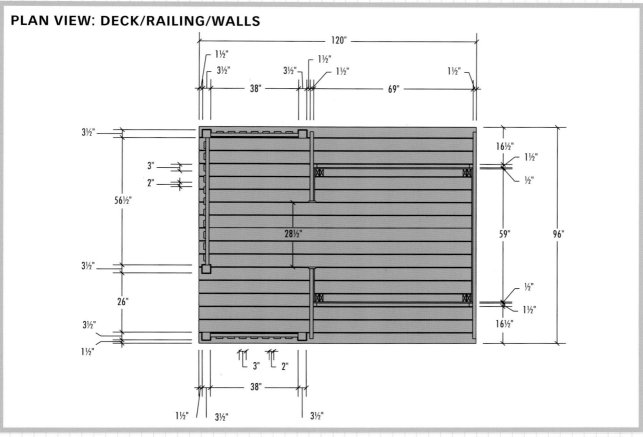

Plan 3: Half-covered Crow's Nest

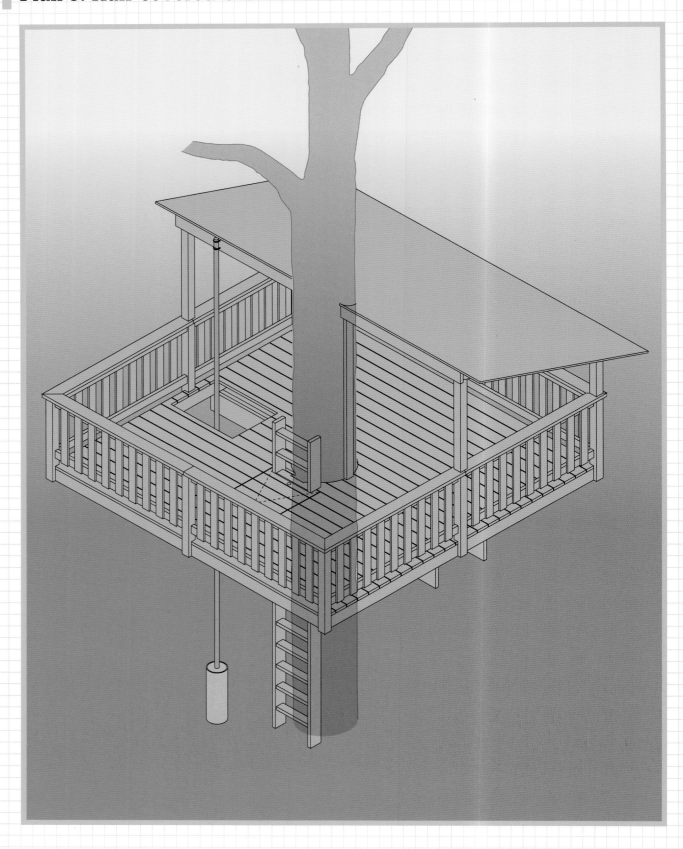

EXPLODED ISOMETRIC

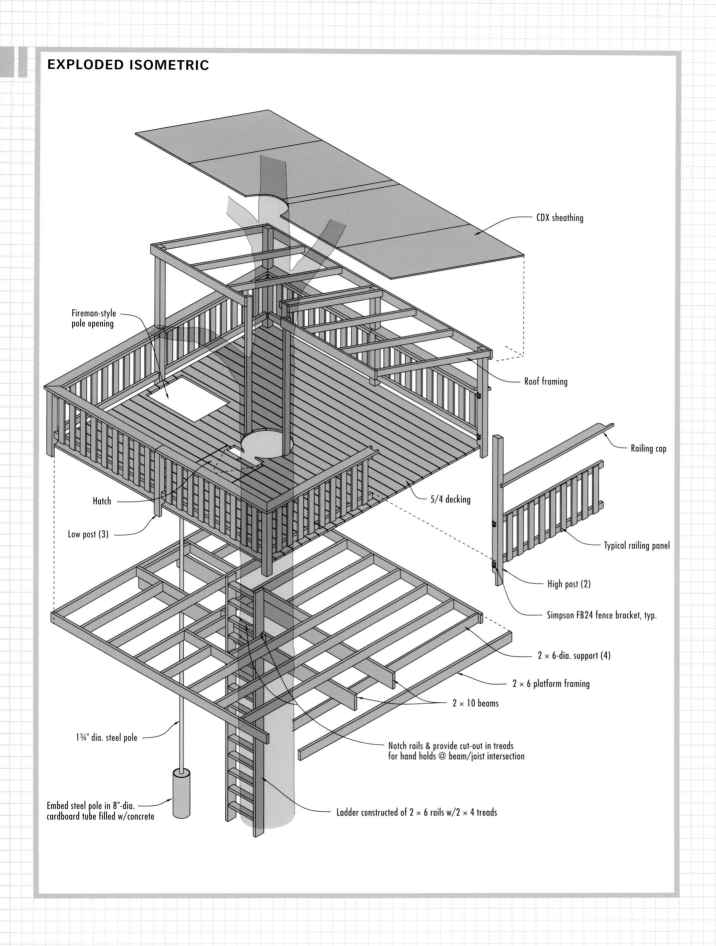

CDX sheathing

Fireman-style
pole opening

Roof framing

Railing cap

Hatch

Low post (3)

5/4 decking

Typical railing panel

High post (2)

Simpson FB24 fence bracket, typ.

2 × 6-dia. support (4)

1¾" dia. steel pole

2 × 6 platform framing

2 × 10 beams

Notch rails & provide cut-out in treads
for hand holds @ beam/joist intersection

Embed steel pole in 8"-dia.
cardboard tube filled w/concrete

Ladder constructed of 2 × 6 rails w/2 × 4 treads

ELEVATION & SIDE

ELEVATION & LADDER

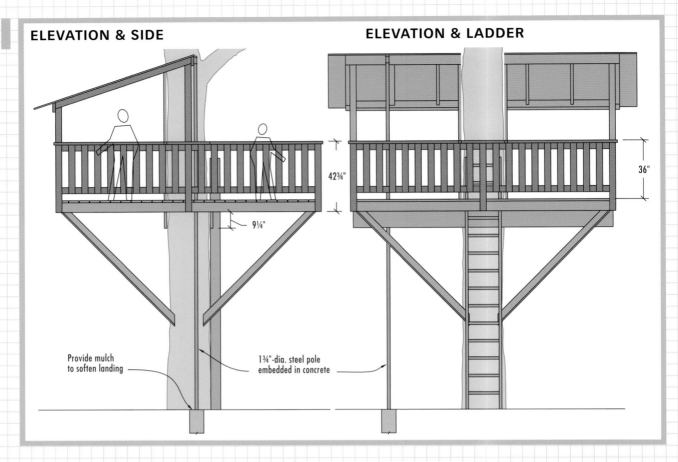

42¾"

36"

9¼"

Provide mulch
to soften landing

1¾"-dia. steel pole
embedded in concrete

SIDE SECTION @ ROOF/RAILING

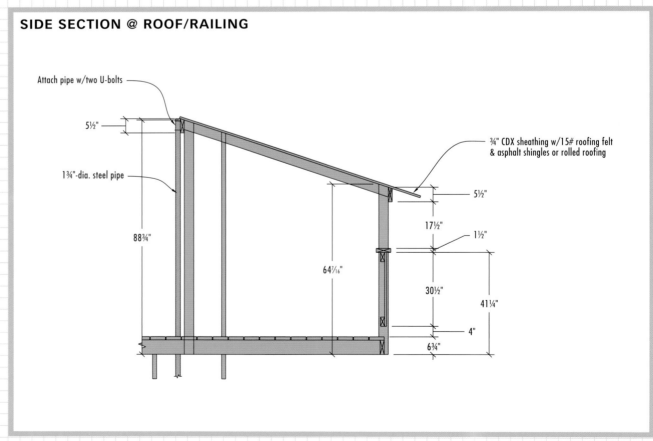

Attach pipe w/two U-bolts

5½"

1¾"-dia. steel pipe

¾" CDX sheathing w/15# roofing felt
& asphalt shingles or rolled roofing

5½"

17½"

1½"

88¾"

64⁷⁄₁₆"

30½"

41¼"

4"

6¾"

PLAN VIEW: PLATFORM FRAMING

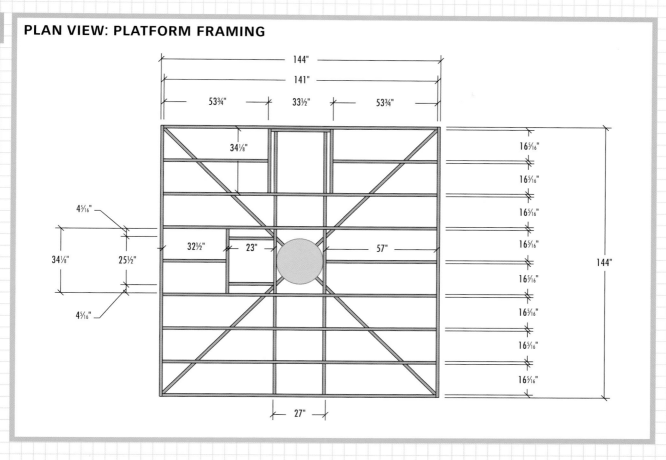

PLAN VIEW: DECKING/RAILING

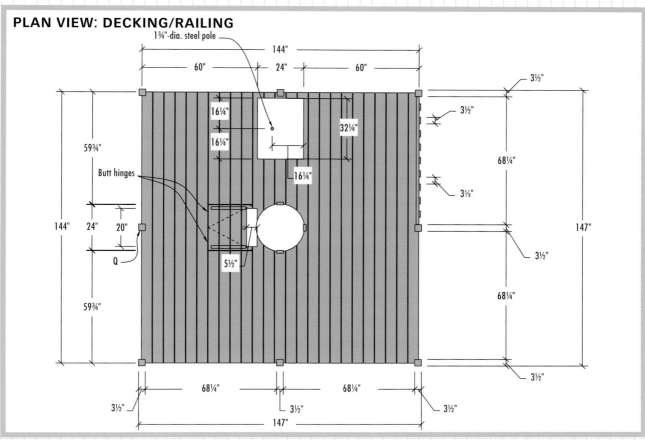

Plan 4: Wraparound Shed on Stilts

EXPLODED ISOMETRIC

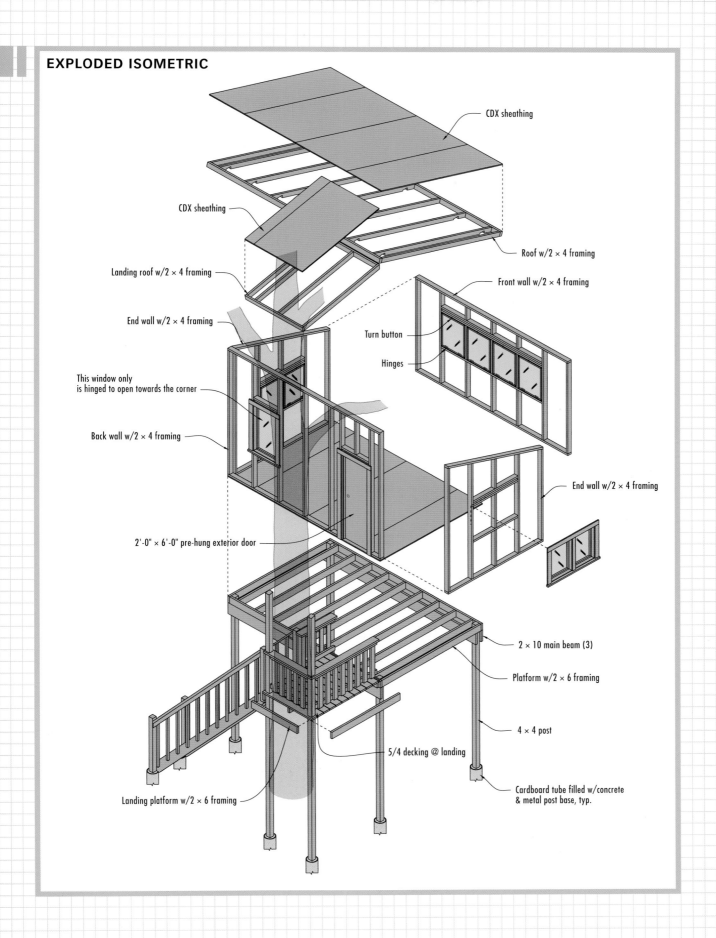

CDX sheathing

CDX sheathing

Roof w/2 × 4 framing

Landing roof w/2 × 4 framing

Front wall w/2 × 4 framing

End wall w/2 × 4 framing

Turn button

Hinges

This window only
is hinged to open towards the corner

Back wall w/2 × 4 framing

End wall w/2 × 4 framing

2'-0" × 6'-0" pre-hung exterior door

2 × 10 main beam (3)

Platform w/2 × 6 framing

4 × 4 post

5/4 decking @ landing

Cardboard tube filled w/concrete
& metal post base, typ.

Landing platform w/2 × 6 framing

ELEVATION: END WALL FRAMING

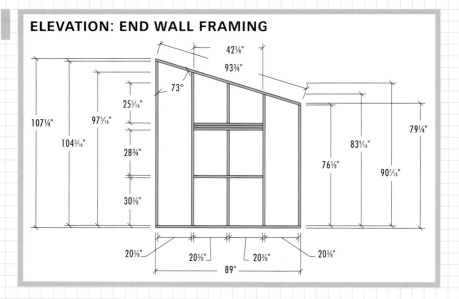

END WALL SIDING

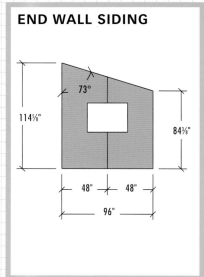

ELEVATION: FRONT WALL FRAMING

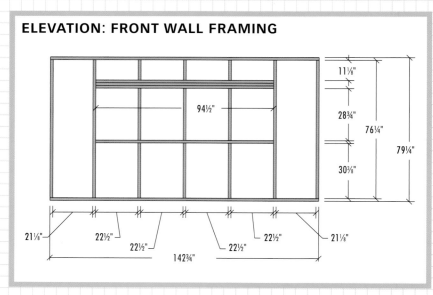

FRONT WALL SIDING

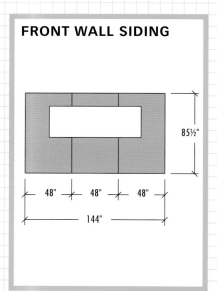

ELEVATION: BACK WALL FRAMING

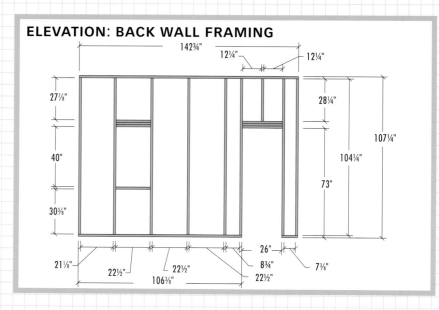

BACK WALL SIDING

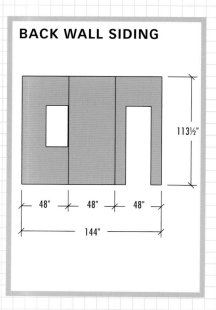

PLAN VIEW: PLATFORM

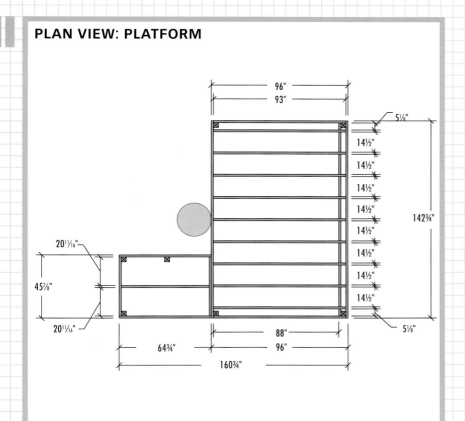

ELEVATION: FRAME/SASH

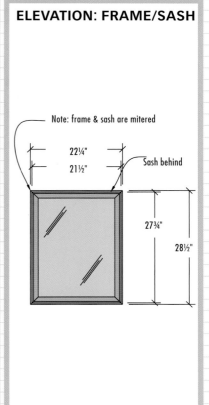

Note: frame & sash are mitered

SIDE SECTION

DETAIL: WINDOW SILL

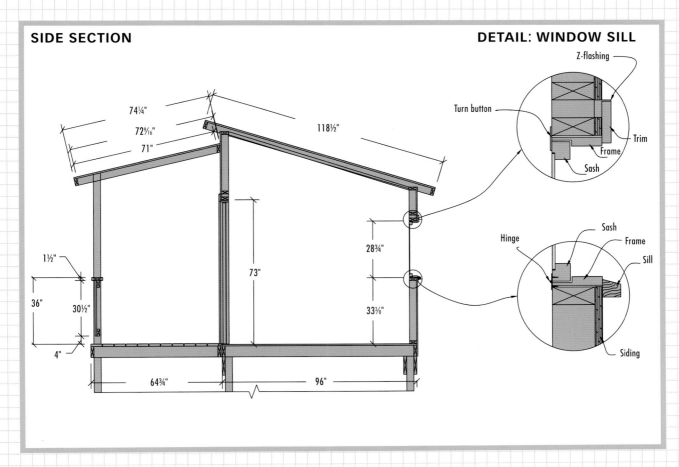

Plan 5: Triangular Tree Hut

EXPLODED ISOMETRIC

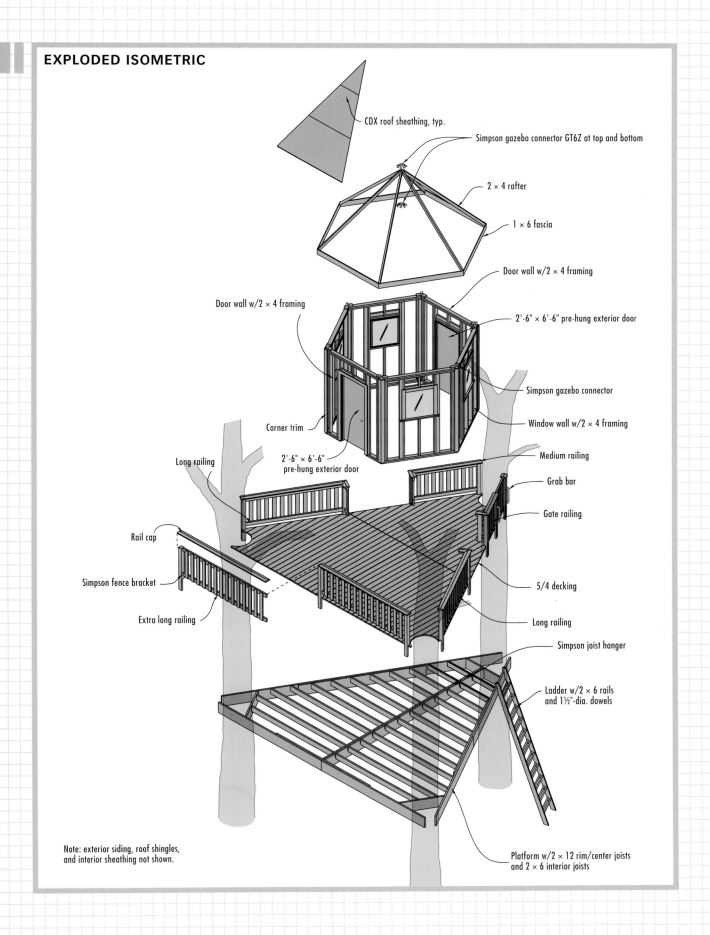

CDX roof sheathing, typ.

Simpson gazebo connector GT6Z at top and bottom

2 × 4 rafter

1 × 6 fascia

Door wall w/2 × 4 framing

Door wall w/2 × 4 framing

2'-6" × 6'-6" pre-hung exterior door

Simpson gazebo connector

Window wall w/2 × 4 framing

Corner trim

2'-6" × 6'-6" pre-hung exterior door

Long railing

Medium railing

Grab bar

Gate railing

Rail cap

Simpson fence bracket

Extra long railing

5/4 decking

Long railing

Simpson joist hanger

Ladder w/2 × 6 rails and 1½"-dia. dowels

Note: exterior siding, roof shingles, and interior sheathing not shown.

Platform w/2 × 12 rim/center joists and 2 × 6 interior joists

WINDOW WALL FRAMING

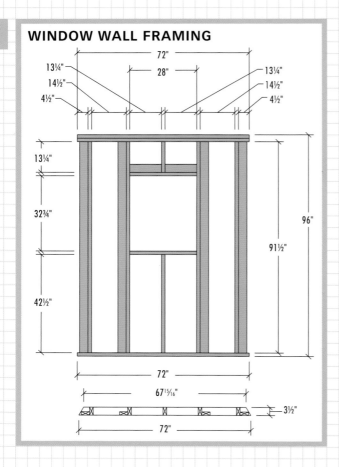

DOOR WALL FRAMING

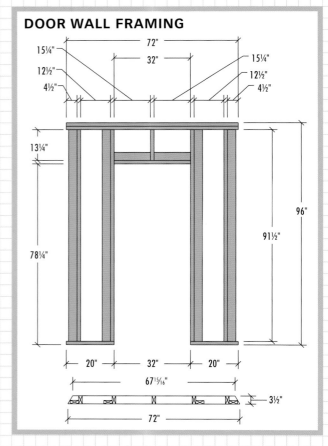

WINDOW WALL TRIM & SIDING

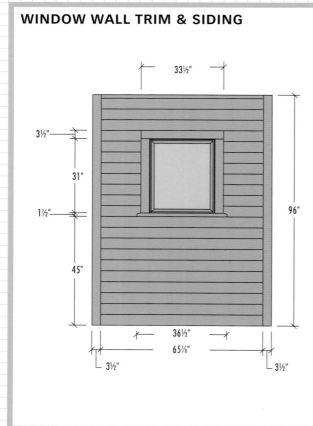

DOOR WALL TRIM & SIDING

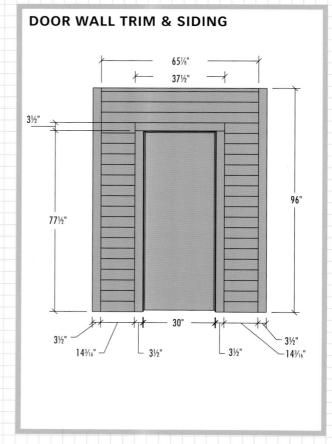

DETAIL: RAIL CAP PROFILE

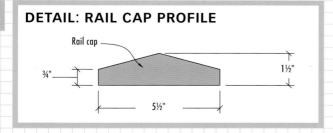

Rail cap

¾"

1½"

5½"

DETAIL: POST NOTCH

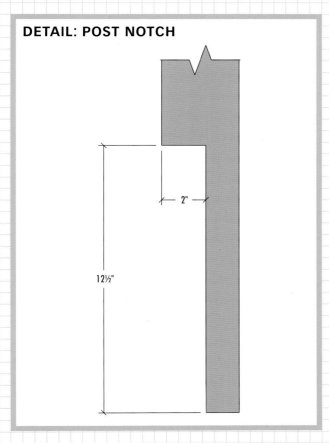

2"

12½"

DETAIL: WINDOW ELEVATION @ INSIDE

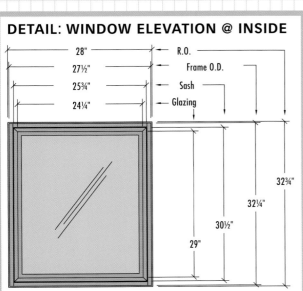

28" — R.O.

27½" — Frame O.D.

25¾" — Sash

24¼" — Glazing

32¾"

32¼"

30½"

29"

DETAIL: WALL CORNER

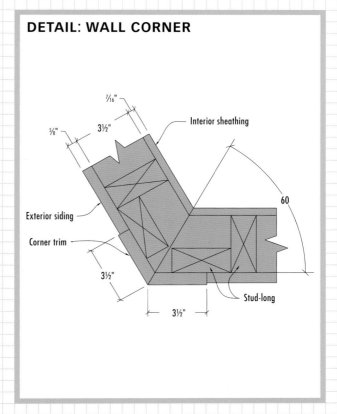

Interior sheathing

7/16"

3½"

5/8"

60

Exterior siding

Corner trim

3½"

3½"

Stud-long

DETAIL: WALL SECTION @ WINDOW

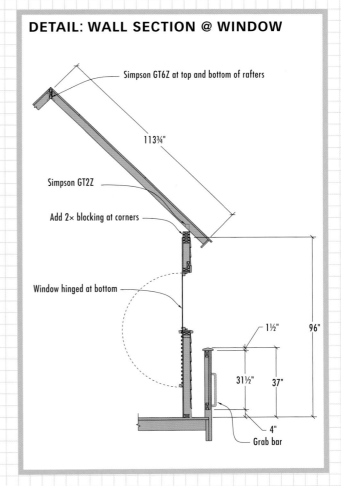

Simpson GT6Z at top and bottom of rafters

113¾"

Simpson GT2Z

Add 2× blocking at corners

Window hinged at bottom

1½"

96

31½" 37"

4"

Grab bar

Plan 6: Four-tree Shanty

EXPLODED ISOMETRIC

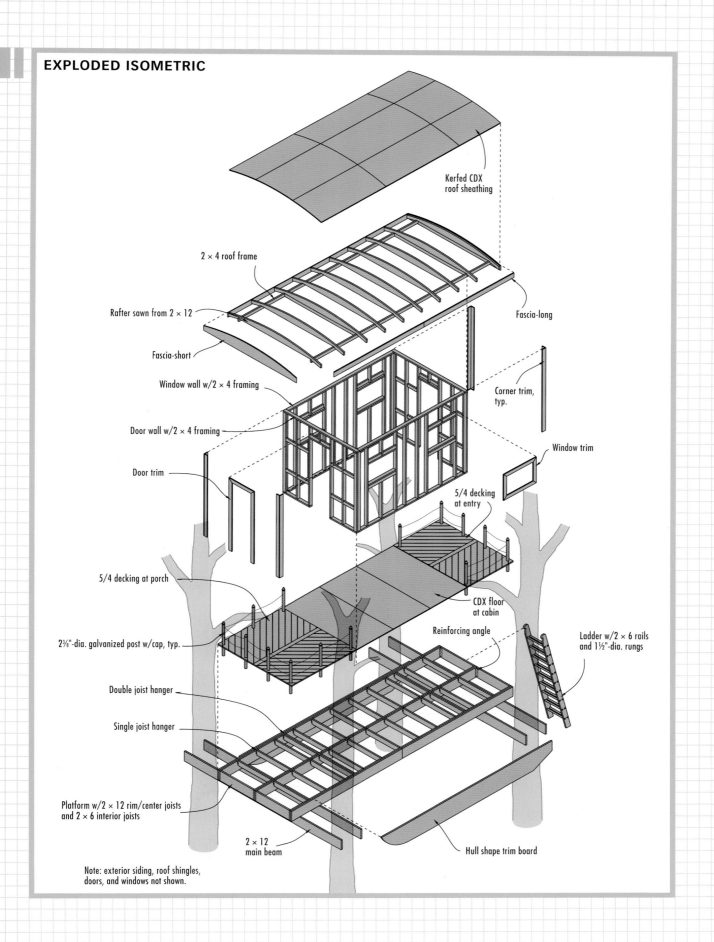

Kerfed CDX roof sheathing

2 × 4 roof frame

Rafter sawn from 2 × 12

Fascia-short

Window wall w/2 × 4 framing

Door wall w/2 × 4 framing

Door trim

5/4 decking at porch

2⅜"-dia. galvanized post w/cap, typ.

Double joist hanger

Single joist hanger

Platform w/2 × 12 rim/center joists and 2 × 6 interior joists

2 × 12 main beam

Note: exterior siding, roof shingles, doors, and windows not shown.

Fascia-long

Corner trim, typ.

Window trim

5/4 decking at entry

CDX floor at cabin

Reinforcing angle

Ladder w/2 × 6 rails and 1½"-dia. rungs

Hull shape trim board

ELEVATION @ FRONT/DECK

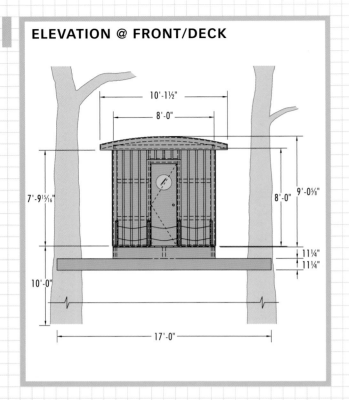

ELEVATION @ BACK/ENTRANCE

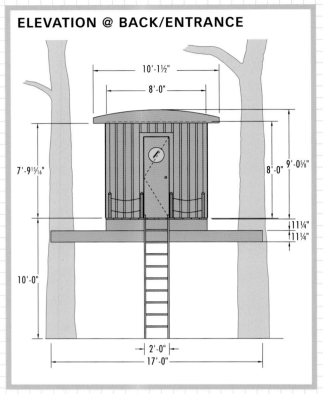

ELEVATION @ SIDE

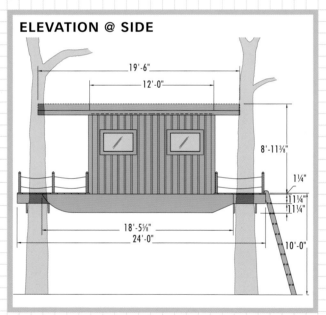

SIDING @ DOOR WALL CORNER

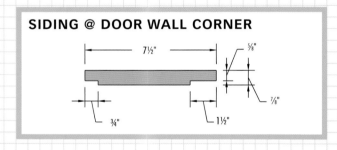

SIDING DETAILS

Typical siding

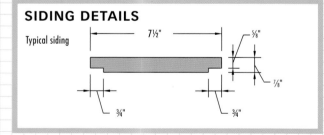

RAFTER DETAIL

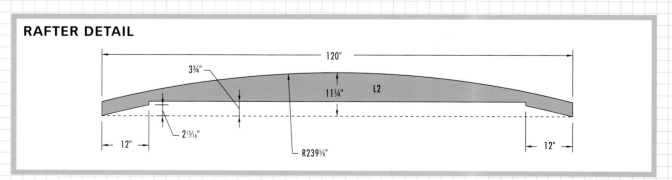

PLAN VIEW: WALL FRAMING ONLY

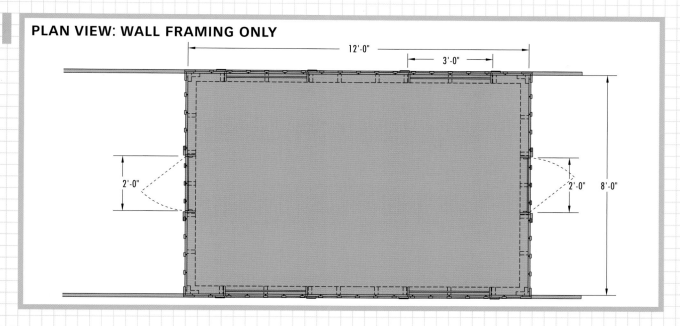

PLAN VIEW: ROOF FRAMING

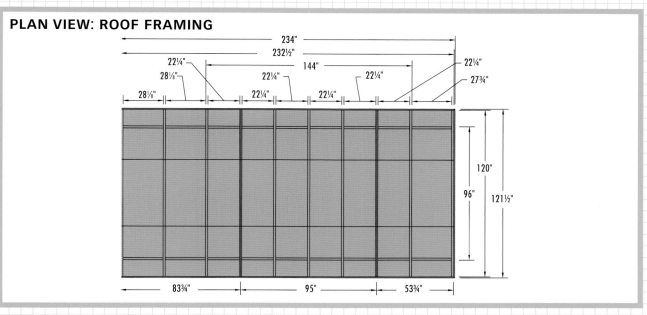

WINDOW WALL FRAMING

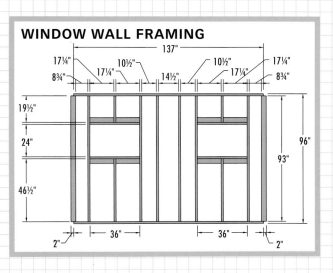

DOOR WALL FRAMING

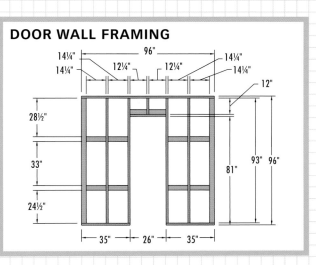

Reference Charts

Metric Conversions

TO CONVERT:	TO:	MULTIPLY BY:
Inches	Millimeters	25.4
Inches	Centimeters	2.54
Feet	Meters	0.305
Yards	Meters	0.914
Square inches	Square centimeters	6.45
Square feet	Square meters	0.093
Square yards	Square meters	0.836
Ounces	Milliliters	30.0
Pints (U.S.)	Liters	0.473 (Imp. 0.568)
Quarts (U.S.)	Liters	0.946 (Imp. 1.136)
Gallons (U.S.)	Liters	3.785 (Imp. 4.546)
Ounces	Grams	28.4
Pounds	Kilograms	0.454

TO CONVERT:	TO:	MULTIPLY BY:
Millimeters	Inches	0.039
Centimeters	Inches	0.394
Meters	Feet	3.28
Meters	Yards	1.09
Square centimeters	Square inches	0.155
Square meters	Square feet	10.8
Square meters	Square yards	1.2
Milliliters	Ounces	.033
Liters	Pints (U.S.)	2.114 (Imp. 1.76)
Liters	Quarts (U.S.)	1.057 (Imp. 0.88)
Liters	Gallons (U.S.)	0.264 (Imp. 0.22)
Grams	Ounces	0.035
Kilograms	Pounds	2.2

Converting Temperatures

Convert degrees Fahrenheit (F) to degrees Celsius (C) by following this simple formula: Subtract 32 from the Fahrenheit temperature reading. Then, multiply that number by $5/9$. For example, 77°F - 32 = 45. 45 × $5/9$ = 25°C.

To convert degrees Celsius to degrees Fahrenheit, multiply the Celsius temperature reading by $9/5$. Then, add 32. For example, 25°C × $9/5$ = 45. 45 + 32 = 77°F.

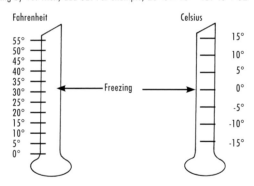

Metric Plywood Panels

Metric plywood panels are commonly available in two sizes: 1,200 mm × 2,400 mm and 1,220 mm × 2,400 mm, which is roughly equivalent to a 4 × 8-ft. sheet. Standard and Select sheathing panels come in standard thicknesses, while Sanded grade panels are available in special thicknesses.

STANDARD SHEATHING GRADE		SANDED GRADE	
7.5 mm	($5/16$ in.)	6 mm	($4/17$ in.)
9.5 mm	($3/8$ in.)	8 mm	($5/16$ in.)
12.5 mm	($1/2$ in.)	11 mm	($7/16$ in.)
15.5 mm	($5/8$ in.)	14 mm	($9/16$ in.)
18.5 mm	($3/4$ in.)	17 mm	($2/3$ in.)
20.5 mm	($13/16$ in.)	19 mm	($3/4$ in.)
22.5 mm	($7/8$ in.)	21 mm	($13/16$ in.)
25.5 mm	(1 in.)	24 mm	($15/16$ in.)

Lumber Dimensions

NOMINAL-U.S.	ACTUAL-U.S. (IN INCHES)	METRIC
1 × 2	$3/4$ × $1 1/2$	19 × 38 mm
1 × 3	$3/4$ × $2 1/2$	19 × 64 mm
1 × 4	$3/4$ × $3 1/2$	19 × 89 mm
1 × 6	$3/4$ × $5 1/2$	19 × 140 mm
1 × 8	$3/4$ × $7 1/4$	19 × 184 mm
1 × 10	$3/4$ × $9 1/4$	19 × 235 mm
1 × 12	$3/4$ × $11 1/4$	19 × 286 mm
$1 1/4$ × 4	1 × $3 1/2$	25 × 89 mm
$1 1/4$ × 6	1 × $5 1/2$	25 × 140 mm
$1 1/4$ × 8	1 × $7 1/4$	25 × 184 mm
$1 1/4$ × 10	1 × $9 1/4$	25 × 235 mm
$1 1/4$ × 12	1 × $11 1/4$	25 × 286 mm
$1 1/2$ × 4	$1 1/4$ × $3 1/2$	32 × 89 mm
$1 1/2$ × 6	$1 1/4$ × $5 1/2$	32 × 140 mm
$1 1/2$ × 8	$1 1/4$ × $7 1/4$	32 × 184 mm
$1 1/2$ × 10	$1 1/4$ × $9 1/4$	32 × 235 mm
$1 1/2$ × 12	$1 1/4$ × $11 1/4$	32 × 286 mm
2 × 4	$1 1/2$ × $3 1/2$	38 × 89 mm
2 × 6	$1 1/2$ × $5 1/2$	38 × 140 mm
2 × 8	$1 1/2$ × $7 1/4$	38 × 184 mm
2 × 10	$1 1/2$ × $9 1/4$	38 × 235 mm
2 × 12	$1 1/2$ × $11 1/4$	38 × 286 mm
3 × 6	$2 1/2$ × $5 1/2$	64 × 140 mm
4 × 4	$3 1/2$ × $3 1/2$	89 × 89 mm
4 × 6	$3 1/2$ × $5 1/2$	89 × 140 mm
6 × 6	$5 1/2$ × $5 1/2$	140 × 140 mm

Liquid Measurement Equivalents

1 Pint	= 16 Fluid Ounces	= 2 Cups
1 Quart	= 32 Fluid Ounces	= 2 Pints
1 Gallon	= 128 Fluid Ounces	= 4 Quarts

Resources

Black & Decker
Portable power tools
www.blackanddecker.com
800-544-6986

Bracketree
Garnier Limb tree brackets
www.treehouses.com/treehouse/construction/
    bracketree.html
541-592-2208

Fehr Bros. Industries
Hardware (cables ties, etc.) for trees:
www.fehr.com/?d=treecare
800-431-3095

**National Resource Center for Health and Safety
    in Child Care**
Recommendations for ground covers under
    play equipment
http://nrc.uchsc.edu/CFOC/HTMLVersion/
    Appendix_V.html
800-598-5437

Red Wing Shoes Co.
Work shoes and boots shown throughout book
www.redwingshoes.com
800-733-9464

Simpson Strong-Tie
Lumber connector hardware
www.strongtie.com
800-999-5099

The Treehouse Guide
On-line treehouse information and links
www.thetreehouseguide.com

Through the Roof
Clear roof sealant
Sashco, Inc.
www.sashcosealants.com
800-289-7290

USP Connectors
Lumber hangers and holddowns
Model TDX2
www.USPconnectors.com
800-328-5934

Photo Credits

Alamy
www.alamy.com
page 12 (top): ©Nina Buesing/Alamy;
page 15 (top right): ©Paul Bradforth/Alamy.

Barbara Butler Artist-Builder, Inc.
www.barbarabutler.com
San Francisco, CA
pages 8, 9 (top), 16 (bottom), 18 (bottom): ©Barbara
    Butler Artist-Builder.

Photolibrary Group Ltd.
pages 10, 11 (top left and right), 13 (bottom left and top):
    ©Juliette Wade/ Garden Picture Library/
    Photolibrary.com;
page 13 (bottom right): ©Mark Bolton/ Garden Picture
    Library/ Photolibrary.com;
page 19 (bottom): ©Ann Cutting/ Botanica/
    Photolibrary.com.

Istockphoto.com
pages 9 (bottom), 145 (bottom left and bottom right):
    ©Mary Martin, istockphoto.com.

Momo Productions
page 105: ©Photonica/Getty Images.

Sergio Piumatti
Richardson, TX
pages 14 (both), 15 (top left, bottom): ©Sergio Piumatti.

Shutterstock.com
page 144.

Andrea Rugg
Minneapolis, MN
pages 11 (bottom), 12 (bottom), 18 (top), 19 (top), 40:
    ©Andrea Rugg.

Jessie Walker
www.jessiewalker.com
pages 16 (top), 17 (both): ©Jessie Walker.

Index